STUNTMEN and DAREDEVILS

Ann Kramer

Galley Press

Designed and produced by
Albany Books
36 Park Street London W1Y 4DE

Copyright © Albany Books 1980

Published in the UK by
Galley Press
Euston Street Freemen's Common
Aylestone Road Leicester LE2
7SS

House Editor: Emma Foa
Design: Ivan Cooper

ISBN 0 86 136046 X

Printed and bound in Hong Kong

Contents

ACKNOWLEDGMENTS

I would like to thank the following individuals and organizations whose help and patience has been invaluable in the preparation of this book:

The Barnstormers Flying Circus
The British Parachute Association
Brian Cartmell Public Relations Ltd
Mary Connors
Jack Cooper
Sue Crosland
Havoc
Eddie Kidd
Richard Laver Publicity
Nine Nine Cars
A D Peters & Co Ltd (for permission to reprint excerpts from *Stunt* by John Baxter)
Rothmans Aerobatic Team
Derek Ware
Joe Weston-Webb
The White Helmets

This page: *A breathtaking display of courage as four men dangle by their feet in a traditional Indian ceremony at Gallup, New Mexico. (Colour Library International)*

Page 4: *Stunting in the theatre – a scene from a 19th century production of* Le pays de l'or *performed at the Théâtre de la Gaîté, Paris. For this remarkable scene, the principal actress rode a specially-constructed bicycle across a rigid cable suspended some 20 ft (6 m) above the stage. (Ann Ronan Picture Library)*

Endpapers: *An enthralled crowd in Valls, Spain, gazes upwards at a sensational human pyramid formed by the Castellers. (Tony Stone Associates)*

Introduction

There is a story about a Hollywood stuntman who was asked to produce the effect of someone being blown up. The director explained that he should fall straight into a container of explosive powder which would then be set alight. The stuntman refused. Surprised, the director exclaimed 'Well you're supposed to be a stuntman aren't you?'

To a great extent the director's attitude mirrors that of the general public. To most people stuntmen are either punch-drunk bruisers with more brawn than sense or impulsive, reckless daredevils prepared to try anything any time with total disregard for personal safety. But in fact, with few exceptions, the reverse is true. Stuntmen in the main, whether in the cinema or in show work, are highly skilled and precise technicians who leave nothing to chance. They operate in what is potentially one of the most dangerous professions of all and their aim is to remain in it, not to sensationally break world records and perhaps die seconds later. The sequel to the original story was that the stuntman suggested a much safer way of doing the stunt with equally sensational effects – a sequel that in fact sums up the craft of the professional stuntman.

Stunting as a highly visual and dangerous form of entertainment goes back to the very earliest days of entertainment itself. And many elements of the modern stunt have their origins in much earlier spectacles. Some 4000 years ago in ancient Crete, the technique of 'bull-leaping' in which an individual somersaults over the back of a stampeding bull was highly regarded. Variations of that stunt have since found their way into circuses and rodeos and today are probably best associated with the Western. The Romans took a delight in producing highly dangerous and spectacular forms of entertainment ranging from gladiatorial combat to chariot racing. The same two elements of highly visual spectacle and of danger continued to weave their way through the travelling fairs and street entertainments of

Above right: *In this scene from an episode of* The Hazards of Helen *(1914–16), stuntwoman Helen Gibson leaps from a moving car onto a travelling box car. Born Rose Wenger, Helen Gibson was typical of the early stunt performers who were prepared to try virtually anything, however hazardous.* (Kobal Collection)

Below right: *A typical mixture of comedy and thrill as the Keystone Kops teeter at the edge of a building. It was in Mack Sennet's Keystone studio that most of the early cinema stunting techniques were born and tested.* (John Topham Picture Library)

medieval Europe into the circuses, music halls and even theatres of more modern times. And running parallel have always been the attempts by individuals to achieve ever more spectacular displays of skill embodied perhaps in the achievements of men such as 'Birdman' Leo Valentin and Evel Knievel.

It was with the advent of cinema that the possibilities for truly spectacular stunting really exploded. In film there were no physical limitations, and a combination of the stuntman's courage and a growing technology coupled with a demand for ever more complex action led to increasing attempts to exploit the possibilities. In the early days of film hazardous action was generally performed by extras keen to earn the odd $3 or perhaps even $5 a day, or by the actors themselves. They took extraordinary risks. Helen Gibson was one of the earliest 'action' performers who was prepared to attempt almost anything. Star of various action serials including *The Hazards of Helen* (1914), her stunts included riding a motorcycle at top speed through a wooden gate, up a station platform, through the open doors of a boxcar, into the air, and onto the open wagon of a moving train.

Above left: Sean Connery in a scene from The Great Train Robbery *(1978). Here performing his own stunts, Sean Connery makes his way along a train travelling at about 50 miles (80 km) an hour. Other actors who have performed their own stunts include Buster Keaton, Harold Lloyd, and Burt Lancaster. (United Artists)*

Below left: A spectacular example of motorcycle stunting. Motorbikes have provided the medium for some of the most dramatic, and dangerous, displays of stunt work. (Spectrum)

But with the growth of the industry and the making of stars it was no longer possible for directors to risk the lives and limbs of their performers and as a result the professional stuntman was born. There have been a number of stars, among them Buster Keaton, Errol Flynn, Douglas Fairbanks, Burt Lancaster and Steve McQueen, who have performed many or all of their own stunts, but in the main from *Intolerance* (1916) to *Hooper* (1978), it has been cinema's small band of professional, and anonymous, stuntmen and women who have been responsible for putting spectacular action into the movies, doubling for the stars when the risks became too great. In fact it is these two aspects – anonymity and the need to be an actor – that distinguish the cinema stuntman from stuntmen in other fields. Although audiences expect remarkable cinema action, very few people have ever heard of or would recognise the names of even the greatest stunt people. By contrast, most people have heard of Houdini or Evel Knievel. Until quite recently, despite their fundamental importance to the movie industry, stuntmen's achievements were recognised only by other professionals and the stars themselves. Likewise, the quite horrifying toll of accidents and deaths was kept well concealed.

Today all that is changing. Since the mid-1960s with the publicly-acknowledged death of stunt flier Paul Mantz and the award of an Oscar, in 1966, to stuntman Yakima Cannutt, stunt people are receiving recognition and film credits. In fact in some ways anonymity is being replaced by myths, legends and mystique. For despite all the planning, all the preparation and all the rigging, stunting in any field is always dangerous. Given the very nature of stunting, risks can only be minimised, they can never be removed.

Falls and Dives

In September 1978 Hollywood stuntman A J Bakunas, aged 27 and veteran of more than 2500 high falls, was killed while attempting a 323-foot (98-metre) fall from a skyscraper for the film *Steel* (1979). His landing rig – an air pad into which air was being constantly pumped and expelled – was faulty and when Bakunas hit it, at an estimated speed of 115 miles (185 km) per hour, the bag collapsed. It is possible that a seam was already damaged. Bakunas later died of internal injuries. Less than three weeks previously, while doubling Burt Reynolds in the film *Hooper* (1978), Bakunas had successfully plunged 230 feet (70 m) from a helicopter onto the same type of pad. In doing so he had, almost incidentally, broken the world's free fall record. In cinema stunting, falls as high as these are a rarity. But falls of anything up to 90 feet (27 m), and sometimes more, are frequently performed by stuntmen. Cinema falls can vary from an apparently simple trip and stumble to the difficult stairfall and extremely spectacular high fall. All of them require precise coordination and a high degree of skill.

Falls as stunts go back to the very earliest days of cinema. Some of the earliest high falls occurred in D W Griffith's *Intolerance* (1916) in which actors were hurled off the walls of Babylon. For these sequences safety nets, an idea borrowed from the circus, were used to catch the falling actors.

The introduction of the high fall also influenced the antics of the early cinema comedians. Actors such as Fatty Arbuckle, Buster Keaton and Harold Lloyd took the simple comic tumble and turned it into a staggering range of falls, leaps and dives, toppling out of windows, off roofs and from other high places. Many of these early actors worked without protective rigging, relying entirely on acrobatic ability for their safety. On one occasion stuntman Dick Grace fell 25 feet (8 m) without any rigging and Buster Keaton, in particular, was renowned for his almost death-defying stunts in which he was protected by his natural acrobatic abilities and innate sense of timing.

As falls became more spectacular it was obvious that some sort of shock absorber was essential. One of the earliest used was the flock or straw mattress, but it had disadvantages. For safety, a particular landing technique was essential and there were other risks too. Filming

Twenty-seven year old cinema stuntman, A J Bakunas, plunges 323 ft (98 m) from a skyscraper for the film Steel *(1979). On landing Bakunas was critically injured and later died of internal injuries.*
(AP Laserphoto)

Safety Last (1923), Harold Lloyd worked 14 feet (4 m) above a platform with mattresses piled on it. The platform was not enclosed and in the event of a fall there was the ever-present risk of bouncing straight off into the street below, as actually happened to a dummy on one occasion.

As the mattress was discarded, other methods were tried and also rejected. Buster Keaton injured himself using a straw-filled pit for a fall from the second floor of a building in *One Week* (1920) and injured himself again using a similar

pit for a 50-foot (15-metre) dive in *Hard Luck* (1921).

For many years the net continued to be the only safety device for high falls. It too had disadvantages. Again it required a specialist landing technique and also had a tendency to bounce an actor back up in front of the camera.

From the 1930s, cardboard boxes began to replace the safety net as a landing rig. And today, for high falls, the box rig is still the preference of most stuntmen. Essentially a box rig consists of a number of cardboard boxes, each measuring 2 feet by 4 feet (.6 m × 1.2 m), stacked on top of each other in layers rather like a brick wall. The height and width of the rig depends on the type of fall. Sometimes flattened cardboard boxes are placed between each layer. The stack is roped together to prevent scattering and may be covered with tarpaulin and mattresses. Where the landing itself is being filmed, the rig can be disguised or set into a pit. It can also be masked. One of the cinema's most spectacular high falls occurred in *Beau Geste* (1936). In this, stuntman Otto Mazette made a dramatic backwards fall

from a tower onto a box rig masked from view by a high wall.

Although the box rig may seem a rather make-shift safety measure, it is remarkably effective. Its success lies in the way the boxes gradually collapse as the faller lands, their collapse absorbing the impact of the faller's body. Most recently air pads have also been used, particularly in the United States. They too are safe, provided the faller lands in the middle of the pad. A landing within 4 feet (1 m) of the edge causes the air pad to collapse, spilling the stuntman onto the concrete. The box rig allows a more flexible landing area.

Today's cinema high fall is an extremely skilled stunt, and for a cinema audience it is always one of the most impressive. High falls divide into two categories – low falls of up to about 30 feet (9 m) – roughly the equivalent of a three-storey building, and high falls of anything more than 30 feet (9 m). Ninety feet (27 m) is generally considered to be the limit of the high fall, but higher falls have certainly been done by stuntmen.

A high fall is not just a topple off. Generally something has preceded the fall, perhaps a fight, and the fall has to be incorporated into the sequence. Before actually 'throwing' the fall, the stuntman not only has to carefully study the route of his fall deciding how to drop and roll, but also has to decide what sort of fall will look most natural given the preceding action.

For a fall of above 30 feet (9 m), specialist

Above left: *Gene Kelly leaps through a window in a scene from* The Three Musketeers *(1948). A natural acrobat and brilliant dancer, Gene Kelly used no double for the stunts in this film, and apparently trained for two months beforehand. (Kobal Collection)*

Below left: *An early stuntman tumbles perfectly over a moving car for a 1928 Metro-Goldwyn-Mayer production. (Kobal Collection)*

Right: *A spectacular high fall by a stuntman at Universal Studios, California. High falls such as these require not only courage but also perfect planning, timing, and body control. (Peter Newark's Western Americana)*

ability in aerial body control is essential and many high fall stuntmen have previous acrobatic or high diving experience. British stuntman Jack Cooper, one of the cinema's most experienced stuntmen, was originally a high diver in aqua shows. He went into the circus where he was catching on a trapeze, and then moved into cinema stunting.

Some of his most notable falls include a 75-foot (22-metre) fall over the side of a ship in *Crimson Pirate* (1951), a fall of about 87 feet (26 m) in the film *Helen of Troy* (1956) and a fall of 84 feet (25 m) for the film *Exodus* (1960). Describing his feelings before a high fall he says that when looking down the box rig looks 'like a postage stamp. It always looks too small.' And that before every fall 'I have a very bad feeling in my stomach . . . the worst point is when you're falling but your feet are still touching. I never jump. I've always done a fall, always believe in leaving my feet behind because I know exactly where the body's going to go. As soon as the feet come clear, the moment they are free, I've got complete control and it's a different feeling . . . it's lovely. Anyone who says it doesn't affect them is a liar or a fool.'

Correct landing technique is vital. Ideally the stuntman aims to land on his back, body spread-eagled over the rig. An experienced stuntman delays the landing position until fairly close to the rig. Jack Cooper mentions that 'from a high fall you've either got to land on your shoulders with your feet going away from you so that in actual fact you've done half a turn . . . in actual fact you hold off . . . I always hold off until I'm about 6 feet (2 m) above the rig and then tuck my head in so that I hit with the shoulders and I unwind wherever possible. If you're going backwards you've got to watch your feet, so that you almost hit flat on your back or seat first and then go back. You're unwinding again. If you go the opposite way you concertina your lungs. In

A stuntman combines two highly dangerous feats – a high fall of at least 30 ft (9 m) from the top of a building plus a fire gag – to produce a very dramatic stunt. (Kobal Collection)

actual fact you've got to be throwing yourself out flat.'

By their very nature, high falls are dangerous and accidents do occur. For his *Crimson Pirate* fall, Jack Cooper had to hit the water flat on his back. Afterwards he spat blood for half an hour and was temporarily paralysed. He was again injured after a 60-foot (18-metre) fall from a rope on the side of a cliff face for the film *Where Eagles Dare* (1968). Unknown to him the mattress on top of his box rig had frozen solid during the previous night. The unforeseen apart, a landing onto the side of a rig, can lead to broken bones, and landing on the side of the body rather than the back can cause serious leg injuries.

Sometimes a fall is made even more complex by the stuntman's need to fall through structures such as doors or windows. One notable example occurs in *The Glass Key* (1942) in which a stuntman doubling for Alan Ladd leaps through a window and drops 17 feet (5 m) through a glass skylight to land 9 feet (3 m) below on a small table covered with crockery and food.

Another example occurs in *It's a Mad, Mad, Mad, Mad World* (1963) in which a stuntman, doubling Spencer Tracy, is thrown off a wire into a tree. The branch for which he grabs breaks and hooks onto a telegraph wire, sliding him down towards a building. The stuntman is carried through a window and into an office, the floor of which collapses, depositing him in the room below.

Despite the use of specially prepared structures such as toffee-glass or plastic windows, and balsa wood for doors, floor and walls, stunts such as these are always dangerous. They require perfect planning, skill and precise timing. The much-filmed stairfall is another highly skilled and specialist stunt. As always, the stuntman has to do two things at once – fall down the stairs without injury and make the fall look as effective and natural as possible.

Stuntwoman Sue Crosland has performed many stairfalls for both cinema and television. She mentions that the main difficulty is to make the fall look natural while at the same time to keep moving. 'Normally, if you fall down by accident, you naturally don't fall all the way down. You would stop unless the stairs were straight and very steep . . . so it is a matter of tucking and pushing yourself off after a while. You've got to relax to a certain extent otherwise you will feel every bump, and you've got to try and fall as naturally as you can.'

As with all cinema stunts, a stairfall is carefully planned and prepared. The shape and route that the stairfall takes depends on the preceding action. The fall may start with a backward launch, the stuntman having climbed the stairs only to be hit or punched when he reaches the top. Or the fall may start with a forward trip or stumble.

The stairs themselves also influence the way in which the stuntman falls. The flight may be straight, curved or spiral and there may or may not be bannisters. Obviously the fall is easier if the stairs are covered, but frequently they are bare concrete or wood. Sue Crosland's most difficult stairfall was one in which she had to fall from the top to the very bottom of an uncovered metal spiral staircase for a television drama series set in a women's prison.

Once the surrounding action has been worked out, the fall itself is entirely up to the stuntman. The stunt itself is never actually rehearsed; it just has to happen and the way in which it does depends on the stuntman's skill. An experienced stuntman will have an exact mental picture of the way in which he is going to fall, perhaps launching backwards over the first few stairs, then hitting the stairs with his shoulder, twisting so that he is facing down the stairs and finishing lying down at the bottom. Although the stunt is not rehearsed, an experienced stuntman will be able to repeat the fall two or three times in exactly the same way.

Probably one of cinema's most spectacular and difficult stairfalls occurs in *The Boss* (1946). For this, three stuntmen – Harvey Parry, Paul

Page 20: *Two stuntmen launch themselves off the top of a waterfall into the swirling waters below. Rehearsing a stunt such as this is virtually impossible; instead the stuntman has to work out a precise routine beforehand and then follow it absolutely.* (*Kobal Collection*)

Stader and Saul Gross – were handcuffed together for a dramatic stairfall.

Although stairfalls are not as dangerous as high falls, some bruising is inevitable as the body is in contact with hard surfaces all the time. Ankles, elbows, knees, hips, kidneys and the base of the spine are particularly vulnerable, and stuntmen generally pad up carefully before a stairfall. But here stuntwomen are at a very real disadvantage as their costumes are often too skimpy to allow for padding. And even with padding, the most successful stairfall is often a painful experience.

High dives are another dangerous area of cinema stunting and in this field too stuntmen have broken world records. One of the most notable high dives occurred in 1970 when British stuntman, Alf Joint, dived a staggering 161 feet (49 m) into the Mediterranean for a television commercial featuring a box of chocolates. Having performed the dive successfully once, he was forced to repeat it and on the second occasion wedged his spine.

Essentially, the aim in a high dive is to enter the water as cleanly and as streamlined as possible. But there is always the danger, not only of making a bad entry, but also of accidentally hitting obstacles such as rocks or overhanging cliffs. In the 1920s stuntman Bobby Dunn, one of the original Keystone Kops, was blinded in one eye when, in a high dive, he hit a matchstick floating in the water.

Sometimes deliberate obstacles are put in the stuntman's path for added effect. In *The Great*

Left: A dramatic feet-first jump into water from the rigging of a clipper for a British television series. Professional stuntmen are not confined to the cinema; television too provides considerable scope for stunting. (BBC Copyright)

Page 21: A stuntman demonstrates a high fall for tourists at Universal Studios, California. There is no special school for stuntmen; a novice entering the profession learns by studying the techniques of other, more experienced stuntmen, techniques that tend to be jealously guarded secrets.   (Syndication International)

Race (1965), stuntman David Sharpe dives some 30 feet (9 m) through the windows of a castle towards the moat below. On reaching the water, he plummets straight through a floating rowboat and down to the bottom of the moat. A stunt such as this one requires not only daring but also absolute physical skill and precise timing.

Outside cinema, the highest regularly performed dives into water are those of the famous professional divers of Acapulco, Mexico. Acapulco Bay is formed by two jutting peninsulas and on the western peninsula is a striking cliff formation known as La Quebrada. The height of the cliffs varies from about 30 to 136 feet (9–41 m) at the highest point. Here the Acapulco divers regularly perform their breathtaking spectacle, diving from the cliffs into a narrow crevice between the rocks below. The depth of the water is never more than 12 feet (4 m) and the dive must be timed to occur on the incoming tide.

Below: *A scene from* Thunder in God's Country *in which a stuntman performs a spectacular leap. The effectiveness of this stunt depends not only on the stuntman's skill but also on the accurate placing of the camera.* (*Kobal Collection*)

Any miscalculation would result in instant death. In order to clear the rocks below, a diver has to fly outwards horizontally for about 20 feet (6 m) before turning into the dive itself.

The Acapulco divers sometimes begin diving when they are no more than eight years old, but, remarkably, accidents are virtually unknown, the divers relying on a well-guarded precision technique that is passed on from generation to generation.

Strangely enough, high falls have never been a particular feature of circus entertainment, perhaps because nightly repetition would destroy their effect. But death-defying dives have certainly been a constant feature. In the 1930s a circus artiste called Aloys Peters regularly thrilled audiences by plunging into space from a height of about 75 feet (23 m) with a noose tied around his neck. His timing was so precise that he would land, unharmed, without even a mark on his neck.

A similar act was performed by Cubanos, 'The Flying Dutchman'. He would leap from a platform onto a trapeze, about 30 feet (9 m) away and lying a little below the platform. As he grasped the trapeze, the bar would break and he would plummet towards the ground some

70 feet (21 m) below. Just before he hit the ground, elastic ropes attached to his ankles and to the platform and invisible to the audience broke his fall.

The idea of a dramatically-arrested fall occurs in the remarkable land dives of the Pentecost Islanders. Every year, in a traditional ceremony, the men of the New Hebrides dive from a tower head-first to the ground. Their fall is broken by vine leaves attached to their ankles. The tower, a flimsy-looking structure, is made entirely of tree trunks and vines and constructed around one single high tree. It stands about 68 feet (21 m) high on the side of a hill, giving a diving height of about 78 feet (24 m). At various heights platforms jut out from the tower rather like diving boards. Long vines are attached to the tower end of each platform and are subsequently tied to a diver's ankles. As the diver sails head-first to the ground, the pressure from the vines snaps the supports of the diving platform. This slows down the diver's fall and as his head actually touches the ground, the tautly stretched vines and the recoil of the tower snap him back onto his feet, unharmed. The whole sequence is timed to a split second and the length of the vines is crucial. Too short a vine would mean a juddering mid-air halt; too long a vine would lead to a broken neck. Here too, accidents are virtually unknown, despite the fact that a diver from the highest platform probably reaches a speed of about 45 miles (72 km) per hour.

Left: *In a version of the so-called death slide, British Corporal Michael Slack slides head down along a cable stretching from the top of London's Tower Bridge, to a point on the ground 450 ft (137 m) away. This particular stunt has a long history, stretching back possibly many hundreds of years. (Syndication International)*

Right: *A sensational dive by one of the world-famous Acapulco divers. Diving from more than 136 ft (41 m) into some 12 ft (4 m) of water, the professional divers of La Quebrada hold the world record for the highest most regularly performed dive. (Brian Cartmell P R Ltd 1979, Harry Ormesher)*

Stunts with Vehicles

In the twentieth century vehicles, whether they be cars, motor bikes, trains or even boats, have provided the medium for some of the most spectacular forms of stunting. Inside the cinema and outside, cars and motorbikes in particular have replaced the horse as vehicles for some remarkable displays of skill, courage and even sheer foolhardiness.

In the cinema, car stunts have thrilled audiences since the days of the silent movies. In the early years Mack Sennett's Keystone Kops in their crazy 'kop wagon' wove their way through some hair-raising stunts, setting the pattern for later more sophisticated car chases and stunts associated with such films as *Bullitt* (1968), *The Italian Job* (1968) and *Hooper* (1978).

The early stunt drivers took extraordinary risks, crashing, rolling and leaping cars with virtually no safety precautions at all. Even by the 1930s no-one was really using a roll-bar — the metal reinforcement that prevents a car from buckling and crushing the driver if it rolls over — and such things as petrol gravity feeds were unheard of. Not even safety harnesses and crash helmets were worn; precautions were primitive in the extreme. Drivers used cushions or even rolled-up overcoats as a crude form of protective padding against impact, relying on split-second reactions to get out of the way of the steering column. To minimise the fire risks, miniature tanks were used that held just enough petrol for the stunt and sometimes the driver's seat was removed and the gear and brake handles sawn off.

Joe Wadham is the senior director of the British stunt company Nine Nine Cars based at EMI Film Studios and a stunt driver with some thirty years experience of films. Describing the way in which he began his career as a stunt driver he says '. . . I was watching a company filming. The car driver was supposed to do a spin . . . not all that clever . . . and I made some remark and the assistant said "if you can do better, do it", so I got in the car, did it and they were quite impressed. It was for one of the old

Above right: *A breathtaking stunt from* The Italian Job *(1968). The film features some marvellous examples of first-class stunt driving, most of which were the work of the great French stunt driver, Remy Julienne. (Kobal Collection)*

Below right: *A motorbike leaps off the road and into the air in a spectacular stunt from* Hooper *(1978). Starring Burt Reynolds as an ageing Hollywood stuntman,* Hooper *is a film about stunting and involved more than 60 stunt people in the making of the film. (Kobal Collection)*

Ealing pictures and I got £3 or £4 at the end of the day.'

From these beginnings Joe Wadham went on to drive in a number of films including *The Blue Lamp* (1949), *Monte Carlo or Bust* (1969), *Those Magnificent Men in their Flying Machines* (1965) for which he built and drove the fire engine in its remarkable chase with an aircraft, and *Robbery* (1967) in which he did the spectacular car chase in the first half of the film. Filmed in the uncleared streets of London, this particular chase was so realistic that Joe Wadham found himself spending a night in the police cells until his director Peter Yates arrived the following morning with a full and satisfactory explanation for the police. It was also on the strength of the chase in *Robbery* and his direction, that director Peter Yates went to the United States to direct *Bullitt*.

Remembering the post-war years of car stunting, Joe Wadham has said '. . . in the old days you couldn't wear crash helmets, the directors wouldn't have it . . . you'd turn up on the film and suddenly they'd say "we want to do a roll". So you'd go to a chippie (carpenter) and borrow a piece of sashcord and tie yourself in with the sashcord . . . Rollbar? What's a rollbar? . . . bit of 2 × 4 in. (50 × 100 mm) timber . . . and you didn't have petrol gravity feed . . . It was chance in those days . . . It was risky, a lot of people got hurt. I've had cars blow up in flames and been dragged out . . . The safety factor is a lot better today but they require more . . . the stunts have got to be more dangerous. If it's not dangerous the public's not interested, they've seen it before.'

Today preparations for car stunting are fairly stringent. Safety harnesses and crash helmets are essential and almost invariably worn. The car itself is prepared in a number of ways depending on the type of stunt. All sharp objects such as mirrors, door handles, window winders, and ashtrays are removed. The windscreen may also be removed but not always. Sometimes a particular film sequence, perhaps a drive through blinding rain, actually calls for the windscreen to be seen. Sometimes also, for a really heavy crash, the windscreen may deliberately be kept in as a safety measure as its presence can actually stop a car from smashing into pieces – first time

round only, however. In addition, a petrol gravity feed system is fitted in which the petrol tank is placed higher than the carburettor, either in the boot or on the roof of the car. Petrol is then gravity fed into the carburettor, by-passing the petrol pump and so eliminating the danger of sparking. Rollbars are also fitted and certain parts of the car are strengthened to withstand stresses. The floor in particular has to be strong as a driver's life may depend on it. For a leap into water the driver has a bottle of oxygen and a breathing apparatus, and two breakaway doors are fitted for easy exit. Occasionally, for some of the truly violent crashes and explosions such as those in *On the Beach* (1958) and the death crash in *Vanishing Point* (1970), a driverless car is used, fitted with impact switches to make it explode when required. The dummy car is linked to a second car driven by a stuntman, towed at speed and then released into the shot.

Ramps are used to roll a car. The length and height of the ramp depends on the stunt. For show purposes the ramp is usually visible to the audience. The car is driven up the ramp at speeds of between 25 to 60 miles (40–96 km) an hour depending on the length of travel and number of rolls required, with the wheels on one side only hitting the ramp. As the height of the ramp increases, the car is pushed over. But the results are not always certain, sometimes the car may even fail to roll over. In films, the ramps tend to be hidden. Their construction consists of

Above right: *As part of a publicity stunt, three members of a British stunt team drive their cars up and off ramps towards a river.* (Features International)

Centre right: *As the cars drop down towards the water, it is worth noting that all three doors on the drivers' side have been removed for easy exit. Note too that the windscreens have not been removed.* (Features International)

Below right: *End of a stunt. The cars are semi-submerged while the drivers, unharmed, start making their way to the river bank.* (Features International)

a long, thin, metal pole about 6 inches (150 mm) in diameter that slides up underneath the car to act as a lever. The wheels never actually touch the pole, the chassis is used to turn the car instead and the driver can line up to his shot with remarkable accuracy.

But despite modern safety precautions the risks can only be minimised, they can never actually be removed. Car stunting is still dangerous and probably always will be. There are numerous categories of car stunts – head-on crashes, side-on crashes, skid crashes, roll-overs, leaps, chases – the list is almost endless. All of them require not only courage but also extremely fast reactions, meticulous planning and split-second timing. In the cinema in particular, car stunting is a precise art – the essential skill lies in absolute precision. Richard Hammatt, junior director of Nine Nine Cars and himself a highly-qualified stunt driver, has explained that '. . . you have to calculate the aftermath of what you are trying to do . . . If you've got to skid a car and put it in a certain position, you've got to visualise where you are going to end up.

Above: *The final scene from* Vanishing Point *(1970) as the film's hero, Kowalski, deliberately crashes into a road block. This remarkable stunt was engineered by stuntman Carey Loftin. A dummy car, loaded with explosives, was used and towed into the shot. (Peter Newark's Western Americana)*

Mentally during the course of that shot, you can almost calculate down to the last few inches where you've got to stop and that is the skill. Anybody can say if you've got the nerve you can jump into a car and roll it, but then the director doesn't just want a roll-over, he wants that car to happen in a certain time at a certain place . . . you've got to be able to do it right . . . and if the cameras are not right, you've got to be able to do it all over again, in exactly the same way.'

Planning and preparation are vital to achieve this accuracy. Whether it is for a stunt show or a film, the stunt itself is worked out quite scientifically. If it is for a film or a commercial, rehearsals may include going through the sequence at, say, three-quarter speed, calculating exactly where the car or cars involved have to be at a certain time. Speeds obviously vary depending on what is called for. A safe speed today is somewhere between 40 and 50 miles (64–80 km) per hour, bearing in mind that when two cars hit each other at these speeds, it results in an 80 to 100 mile (129–161 km) an hour impact. Once the director calls 'action', the stuntman just has to go, and more often than not he only has one chance to get it right, few companies have a back-up car standing by.

Car stunting has definitely claimed its victims, and in recent years these have included such people as the great French stunt driver Gil Delamare who was killed in a car crash in the 1960s. Another fatality occurred in 1970 when John Bell, stunt driver with the British Destruction Squad stunt team was killed. As part of a dramatic mock accident, Bell was being towed along the ground by a car. Members of the audience, thinking it was a real accident, rushed out. The driver swerved to avoid them, and Bell crashed into a barrier post fatally injured.

Fortunately today fatalities are fairly rare,

more usual are broken arms or broken legs. But when an accident does occur, it is rarely through lack of skill or through lack of preparation; it is more likely to be caused by the unforeseen. Sometimes it is a mechanical failure. Filming *The Green Helmet* (1961) Joe Wadham was driving through a mountain pass. Going fast round a sharp left-hand bend with a 400 foot (122 m) drop, the gear box suddenly failed. The car ploughed through a low granite wall for a distance of 12 or 14 feet (3–4 m) before finally being brought to a shattering halt, half the car hanging over the cliff. Inside the car Wadham and his co-driver could hear the sound of petrol escaping. Fortunately both managed to get out before the car either blew up or plunged over the side of the cliff.

More recently stunt driver Mark Boyle did a

Below: *A car hurtles into the sea in a shot from* Grand Prix *(1966). Here too a dummy car and dummy driver have been used. In this case, the car was fired from an air cannon.* (*Kobal Collection*)

spectacular car stunt for *The Big Sleep* (1978) in which he drove a Rolls-Royce off a pier into about 16 feet (5 m) of water. On the way to the pier the car had to hit some scaffolding and as it did, a freak accident occurred – a brick went through the windscreen. As the car hit the water, the doors were jammed shut and water poured in through the windscreen knocking Boyle's breathing apparatus out of his mouth. Fortunately, being a professional, he waited until the car had settled into the mud, then knocked a window out and escaped unharmed, despite having been under water for probably some 40 seconds.

Stuntman Jack Cooper also had a near-miss in *The Damned* (1961). Doubling Oliver Reed, he had to drive an old XK120 Jaguar onto and over a bridge into about 18 feet (5 m) of water. As always, he prepared the stunt meticulously beforehand, screwing an aqualung under the floor, rigging the door so that it could be pulled off on the driver's side and actually going into the water to check for possible obstacles. But for some inexplicable reason he forgot to put his safety harness on; as it turned out this was fortunate. Describing the incident he says '. . . I was sitting in the car with the engine running . . . and the first assistant came up and said "I don't want to tell you to go Jack" and I said "I don't want to go" . . . it was that feeling again . . . and I said "I've forgotten something . . . Oh Christ, I've forgotten my safety straps" . . . I jumped out of the car and took the seat out and said "I'll go without the seat" . . . so in actual fact as I drove down the road I was sitting on the floor to get myself low. I came in over the bridge swerving this car because I had to make it look as if it was being driven by someone who was dying from radiation. We'd built the rails of wood and had taken one out of them and I had to go through this spot exactly at nearly 60 miles (18 km) an hour, and I stabbed the brake and turned the car and as soon as I'd got it lined up, checked it round the opposite lock to bring the car up straight so it wouldn't roll – this is all in split-second time – and then I had it in second gear and stabbed my foot down on the accelerator to try and keep the nose up . . . it went through the rail like a bullet, and it lifted and gradually nose-dived over. When it hit the water, I remember holding onto the wheel but not sitting on anything . . . I felt Bang . . . and I was still waiting for the car to hit the bottom . . . By then I'd smacked my chin (on the windscreen) and it was on the bottom, it went in so quick and clean, and I could feel the water rushing past . . . and I was thinking I was still going down. In actual fact the car was falling in on top of me. Vaguely I remember I could see the sand and I thought "Jesus" and struggled to get back into the cab where the aqualung was but couldn't because of the pressure of rushing water so I decided to try and push out. I thought I had two divers standing by to pull me clear but in actual fact they had been waiting in the speed boat to watch the car come off the bridge and the tide was running so fast that they had drifted something like 200 feet (61 m) down river . . . I remember just feeling as I pushed out, I felt something get hold of my feet and I kicked clear . . . I had a life jacket, a Mae West, and I remember breaking the seal and it blew . . . and I don't remember anything after that.' The whole experience probably lasted no more than 50 seconds. Jack Cooper found out later that it was likely that the windscreen had saved his life. This was because as the car fell upside down the windscreen, before collapsing, probably allowed a momentary stop that enabled him to get clear.

Since the early years of the twentieth century the motorbike too has been a popular stunting vehicle. During the 1920s and 1930s the Wall of Death and the Globe of Death were popular spectacles associated with fairs and motorbike shows. The Wall of Death consisted of a wooden 'pit' some 14 feet (4 m) high. Inside, motor cyclists tore around the walls, climbing up and

Left: Jack Cooper, doubling for Oliver Reed, drives a car through railings and into water for a stunt in The Damned *(1961) that nearly turned into a disaster. (Jack Cooper)*

Page 34: A thrilling spectacle as a cyclist performs a complete loop the loop in front of an amazed audience at Olympia, Paris in 1903. (Mary Evans Picture Library)

down, and being held in place by centrifugal force. The Globe of Death worked on much the same principal.

Even today audiences are still more likely to associate motorcycle tricks with stunt shows and displays than with cinema stunting. In recent years the man who has probably done more to popularise death-defying forms of motorbike stunting is American daredevil Evel Knievel. Born in Butte Montana in 1938 he has made some 300 motor cycle jumps over ever-increasing obstacles ranging from trucks and buses to a highly-publicised but abortive attempt to leap the Snake River Canyon in a rocket in 1974. An extraordinary showman, Knievel has probably broken most of the bones in his body during his remarkable career, one of his most spectacular crashes being at Caesar's Palace, Las Vegas in 1968 when he attempted a 150-foot (46-metre) leap over a fountain. As a result of this attempt he ended up with a broken back, hip, and pelvis but some 15 months later went on to successfully leap his bike over 19 cars, which was then a record. Knievel has been described by some journalists as a 'ballistic cripple' and it is hard to know what motivates him. Certainly he falls into the category of the barnstorming daredevil, challenging death in the most flamboyant way possible, rather than into the category of the professional cinema stuntman one of whose main aims is to avoid injury.

Evel Knievel's exploits have inspired a host of imitators. One in particular is 20-year-old British motorbike stunter Eddie Kidd who by 1979 held the world record for ramp jumping – a distance of 190 feet (58 m) over 14 double decker buses. His other exploits include a spectacular leap over a ravine more than 80 feet (24 m) wide and 80 feet (24 m) deep for the film *Hanover Street* (1979).

Although this type of show stunting is in many ways a far cry from the world of the cinema stuntman, the same degree of planning and accuracy is essential. It is a highly dangerous area in which the enthusiastic amateur can only too easily be injured or killed and which has also claimed a large number of professionals as well. Eddie Kidd himself has said that despite his daredevil image, after his early years of self-

acknowledged foolhardiness, he knows his limits and is now no longer prepared to kill himself for the sake of a world record, or for the sake of attempting the impossible. He plans and rehearses each stunt calmly and meticulously with nothing left to chance, and as a result has so far remained reasonably unscathed.

In a different category but no less spectacular are the displays of precision riding and motorcycle skills put on by such teams as The White Helmets, The Royal Signals Motor Cycle Display Team. First formed in 1927 the team, mounted on Triumph motorbikes, puts on a stunning display of tricks ranging from ramp jumping over cars, bikes, and even people, to leaps through burning hoops and remarkable bike-back acrobatics. Months of careful practice go into producing a display and perfect timing and coordination are the keynotes to its success.

Like car stunts, motorcycle stunts fall into almost endless categories. For the audience one of the most impressive is the 'wheelie' in which the bike is ridden on its back wheel only. It looks dramatic but in fact is not particularly difficult to perform. The rider sits well back, yanks the throttle back and brings the bike up with his hands. From then on the stunt requires a combination of perfect balance and a constant speed. To some extent the much more dangerous

Page 35: *Evel Knievel, the American daredevil, shown here in front of his rocket-powered machine, Sky Cycle X-2, in which he made an abortive attempt to leap Snake River Canyon in 1974.* (*Syndication International*)

Left: *British daredevil and motorcycle stunter, Eddie Kidd, jumps his motorbike over fourteen double decker buses to achieve a world record as the only person to leap such a distance on a bike, and retain control.* (*Mel Bush Organisation Ltd*)

Page 38: *A member of The White Helmets, the British Royal Signals Motor Cycle Display Team, brings his motorbike perfectly through a fire jump. No protective clothing is worn for this act, and even in the most successful fire jump clothes, and eyebrows are invariably singed.* (*Tony Stone Associates*)

ramp jump works on the same principal, certainly as far as take-off goes. A jump from a ramp through, say a hoop of fire, plate-glass window, or even over a line of parked cars, depends for its success on the right speed being maintained. Hesitation before a leap can be fatal as it automatically leads to a lessening in speed and momentum. On landing from a jump, the bike must be brought down back wheel first.

The motorcycle has also featured dramatically in film and television stunting. Here, as always with film stunting, the skills involved are not just those of courage and mastery of the bike but also the ability to incorporate the stunt into the whole of the action surrounding it. Richard Hammatt performed a particularly hazardous stunt for a television commercial featuring road safety. It involved driving a motorbike smack into a stationary vehicle at a speed of about 40 miles (12 km) an hour. In addition to the crash, Hammatt also had to catapult himself off the bike onto the bonnet of the car, then leave the car and roll down into the road. As he describes it himself '. . . you talk it over with the director about where the cameras are going to be and then it's down to you, because it's your safety

Above: A stunt within a stunt. In this scene from The Gumball Rally *a visual joke is created as a motorcycle stuntman crashes into a billboard straight into the path of a paper train. (Kobal Collection)*

Page 39: Setting up a stunt. Members of the British Motobirds check ramp and support a plate-glass window in readiness for a publicity stunt. Seconds later one of the team's motorcyclists crashes through the plate glass window. In a stunt like this it is vital to achieve the correct speed. Failure to do so may mean that the front wheel does not shatter the glass sufficiently for the cyclist to pass through unharmed. (Joe Weston-Webb)

you are taking into account . . . The moment you set off to do a shot you are talking mentally and verbally to yourself . . . you've got 10 feet, 5 feet, 4 feet (3–2–1 m), bang, hit, clear, tuck in, twist, and then that's it . . . you cannot rig . . . once you've made that move and you've set the stunt in motion, you're past the point of no return . . . with motorbikes it's so easy to snap a neck . . . nine times out of ten when motorcyclists are killed they don't die until the ambulanceman takes off the helmet.'

The High Fliers

In the field of stunting, aerial work is probably the most spectacular of all, and certainly the most dangerous. More professional stuntmen have been killed in this field than in any other, and the list of injuries and disabilities is almost endless. But by the same token, aerial work has probably attracted some of the most courageous and flamboyant characters in the history of entertainment.

Aerial acts in the circus are always stunning. Like it or not, the appeal almost definitely lies in their danger, for despite the presence of safety nets, high wire and trapeze acts are extremely hazardous even for the most experienced artistes.

The trapeze acts are relatively new in the history of the circus. The flying trapeze itself was invented in the mid-1800s by the great French circus artiste Léotard. At that time even the fixed trapeze bar was a dangerous novelty, and Léotard astounded audiences by the introduction of a moving bar. Basically Léotard's act consisted of a mid-air transfer from one moving trapeze to another, the second trapeze being set in motion by his father. Léotard used no safety net, only a mattress on the ground below. The safety net was not introduced until about 1871.

Today Léotard's act seems very simple, but at his debut in Paris in 1859 it caused such a sensation that Léotard – the first ever man on the flying trapeze – was paid the unheard of sum of 500 francs a day.

A host of imitators followed Léotard's success and trapeze work became more and more spectacular. Léotard's most notable successors included the great Alfredo Codona, the first flying trapeze artiste to consistently perform a triple somersault, and his wife Lillian Leitzel.

Codona is considered by some to have been the greatest flying trapeze artiste of all time. In 1920, after three years' hard effort, he first successfully performed his triple somersault at the Chicago Coliseum. It was a remarkable achievement and a feat that, before Codona and even since, has caused the death of many trapeze artistes. Codona himself estimated that during the sequence of somersaults he was probably travelling at some 60 miles (95 km) per hour, and that it was instinct and experience only that enabled him to come out of the third somersault sufficiently conscious to be able to grasp the catcher's hand.

To the audience below, the sheer grace and apparent ease with which a trapeze artiste flies through the air makes the act seem very simple. But aerial work is far from simple. An aerialist's life depends on training, experience and absolute coordination of timing and movement. It takes considerable courage to launch into the air, but

once there, instinct and experience take over. Speed can be regulated to some extent. By tucking up the body the aerialist can move a little faster; by stretching out slightly, the body can turn more slowly. But there is very little time in which to perform these manoeuvres. Nor is there time for a flier to look around for the catcher; he must just be there, in the right position, and the two must be perfectly synchronised.

Conditions inside the big top also add to the dangers of an aerialist's work. During a performance, the top of the tent becomes extremely hot and temperatures have been known to reach 132°F (55°C). In turn this leads to sweating, slippery hands, and the risk of a missed catch.

To the audience, the safety net looks reassuring. But a bad landing into a net can be just as dangerous as falling directly onto the floor. Many performers have been seriously injured or even killed because they did not land correctly – a correct landing consisting of 'balling up' the body and landing on the shoulders, legs in the air and knees stiff.

Accidents are rarely due to lack of skill. More usually they occur because of some unforeseen mechanical failure, or because, perhaps inexplicably, an aerialist has a mid-air change of mind.

In contrast to trapeze acts, high-wire work goes back a long way. For hundreds of years, tightrope walking has been a popular spectacle at fairs or circuses, and tightropes have been stretched across all manner of places – rivers, gorges and from one church steeple to another. And at various times extraordinary acrobatic

Left: Burt Lancaster in a still from Trapeze *(1956). Originally a circus acrobat, Burt Lancaster did most of his own trapeze work for this film, using no double. In fact until Lancaster was into his fifties he did most of his own stunt work. (Kobal Collection)*

Below: An early rope dancer of the 16th century. High-wire or tightrope acts go back hundreds of years in the history of entertainment and are perennial favourites in the circus. (Mary Evans Picture Library)

LE DANSEUR DE CORDE

D'APRÈS UN RECUEIL D'EMBLÈMES DU XVIᵉ SIÈCLE

(BIBLIOTHÈQUE DE L'ARSENAL)

feats have been performed on the tightrope. The 17th and 18th centuries saw a number of notable tightrope walkers, one of the most famous being Jacob Hall. He is mentioned by Samuel Pepys in his diaries and was renowned for his ability to dance on the wire.

across. The following year he crossed Niagara again, this time on stilts.

Other great wire walkers include Con Colleano, the first man to perform a forward somersault on the wire, and the remarkable Wallendas. The Wallendas made their debut in 1928 and

Above: *Blondin, probably the most famous of all tightrope walkers. In 1859 he became the first man to cross Niagara Falls on a tightrope, an achievement that he repeated several times.* (*Mansell Collection*)

But the most famous of all wire-walkers was the Frenchman Jean François Gravelet, better known as Blondin, who in 1859 became the first man to cross Niagara Falls on a tightrope. Blondin not only crossed once but several times – once blindfolded, once carrying a man on his back, and once pushing a wheelbarrow. On one occasion he even took a stove with him, sat down, cooked and ate an omelette half way

since that time members of the troupe have astounded audiences with their skill and daring. They are particularly well known for their sensational three-tier act for which they hold the world record. Two members of the troupe, carrying steel balancing poles, cross the wire on foot. A third member stands on a chair balanced on a pole between them, and a fourth person stands on the shoulders of the third. It is an extremely perilous act in which one slip or miscalculation could prove fatal.

One aerial act that never fails to excite an audience is the human cannonball. The performer climbs down inside the muzzle of a

cannon, an explosion occurs, and the performer flies out in a cloud of smoke to land in a safety net perhaps 100 feet (30 m) away.

British stuntwoman Mary Connors is not only a highly proficient motorcycle stunter but also regularly performs a human cannonball act. The cannon she uses has been specially built and requires an explosives license but its actual construction is a trade secret. The muzzle is 24 feet (7 m) long, high and steep, and is a bare 18 inches (458 mm) wide on the inside. Describing the procedure she says '. . . you slide right down to the bottom and become completely and absolutely braced solid . . . the most dangerous bit is to get into the cannon because as you're getting down the tube, if it goes . . . it would just chop your legs off, it could literally chop you in half . . . you've just got to get in and get down as quickly as possible . . . Then you're shot up the barrel and as soon as you feel the air you have to look for the net and get ready to dive into it.'

Describing her feelings before a performance, Mary says '. . . I've never ever got used to it . . . I've done it hundreds of times and never happily got into it without thinking about it . . . but once they start the count-down, once you're in there, you've just got to do it because you can't really get out.'

Inside the cannon is a platform specially designed to take some of the strain off the legs which are particularly vulnerable. Mary Connors herself has permanently damaged the tendons of her knees from shock. It is a gruelling experience at the best of times, and on one occasion, filming a commercial, Mary was forced to repeat the shot twelve times in one day, an experience which left her barely able to walk. Despite the risks, the attraction for Mary, as for many stunt people, lies in 'being able to do something that everybody else wouldn't dare to do, and being able to make yourself do it.'

The introduction of manned flight opened up a staggering range of stunting possibilities. During the 1920s in Europe and the United States, aviation was the rage of the day. Pilots returning from the war bought themselves war surplus planes and their daredevil stunting became a standard feature of summer 'air circuses'.

These were the days of the 'barnstormers', pilots whose daring and aerial skills have become almost legendary. At county fairs they competed against each other to perform ever more dangerous stunts, swooping low over stunned crowds before using the skies as a backcloth for their aerobatics. In those days navigational aids were virtually unknown; the pilots found their way by recognizing landmarks such as roads and railways and deaths were not uncommon.

Some of the barnstormers made their way to California where Hollywood was quick to see the potential of aerial stunting. Men such as Ormer Locklear, Bob Rose, Al Wilson, Al Johnson, and Dick Grace were just a few of the leading stunt pilots.

Known as 'the man who walked on wings', it was Ormer Locklear who pioneered many of the early aerial stunts. A remarkable performer, he had a reckless courage that drove him on almost relentlessly to attempt ever more dangerous

Page 45, above: *The Great Wallendas performing on the high wire at the Circus World Championships in 1977. Their sensational performances demand not only courage but also absolute precision and expertise. (Nick Birch)*

Page 45, below: *Karl Wallenda, at the age of 66, astounds an audience as he makes his way across a tightrope high up in a 150-ft (46-m) high stadium in St Louis, USA. For this performance, Wallenda used no safety net. Half-way along the tightrope, he stopped and stood on his head. (Associated Press)*

Above right: *A stunning aerial act in the Civic Center Plaza in Chicago, Illinois. In the field of stunting and of circus entertainment, aerial acts have probably claimed more victims than any others. (Syndication International)*

Below right: *British stuntwoman Mary Connors flies out of a cannon in a puff of smoke. This particular stunt is extremely dangerous. Not only is the exit from the cannon itself hazardous but also a bad landing in the net can lead to serious injuries or even death. (Joe Weston-Webb)*

stunts. He made wing-walking an art, and in 1919 made the first public mid-air transfer from one plane to another. Filming *The Skywayman* (1920) Locklear was killed shooting the final and most dangerous sequence – a deliberate spin from which the plane never emerged. Also killed in the crash was Milton 'Skeets' Elliott, another great stunt pilot.

These early stunters took extraordinary risks. Until the mid-1920s parachutes were never worn – Locklear himself never considered them to be very safe – and often the only safety device was a rope attached to a strut and tied around the stuntman's ankle. If he fell, he hung head-down until he was able to clamber back onto the plane.

Most of the stunts took place at about 60–80 miles (96–129 km) per hour, and the high winds caused by the forward movement of the plane could literally tear a stuntman's clothes off his back. The early bi-plane stunts fell into various categories – wing-walking, mid-air transfers, air-to-ground transfers, rope work and the aircraft crash. All were dangerous and all required remarkable skill and precision.

A mid-air transfer could be achieved by climbing up, or down, into the second plane. In the first method, the stuntman climbed out of the cockpit, walked along the lower wing, up onto the top wing, and grasped the wing-skid of the plane above. In the second he transferred down to the second plane by means of a rope ladder. The ladder could also be used to transfer from the aircraft to another moving object such as a car or train. Stunting on a rope was extremely difficult as the high winds caused it to twist and

Left: *Mary Connors again flies through the air, this time propelled by a giant catapult, in an unsuccessful attempt to get to the other side of the River Avon, Bristol, England.* (*Joe Weston-Webb*)

Right: *Fraulein K Paulus, a pioneer parachutist at the turn of the century, here still attached directly to a balloon before releasing her parachute.* (*Mansell Collection*)

turn in all directions. It was only too easy for a stuntman's strength to give out, particularly if the stunt had to be repeated, and in 1925 stuntman Gene Perkins was killed while attempting the particularly hazardous aircraft-to-train transfer.

The aircraft crash is probably the most spectacular aerial stunt and some of the best-known names associated with it are Dick Grace, who formed the notorious 'Squadron of Death', Paul

Below: *The American Clem Sohn, one of the greatest 'birdmen' in a long history of birdmen. Until his death in 1937, Clem Sohn performed at air displays throughout the US, England and France. His usual practice was to jump from 9000 ft (2743 m) then to use his home-made canvas wings stretched between arms and knees to glide down to about 1000 ft (304 m) when he would open his parachute. Performing at Vincennes in 1937, he was killed when his feet became entangled in his parachute.* (John Topham Picture Library)

Above: *American cyclist, Bryan Allen, pedalling frantically in the tiny cockpit of his Gossamer Albatross, makes the first ever man-powered flight across the English Channel on June 12, 1979. (Aspect Picture Library)*

Mantz and Frank Tallman. Some of the best examples of aircraft crashes occur in William Wellman's *Wings* (1927), probably the best-produced flying film of that era. Grace himself was hired for three of the most dangerous stunts – a crash landing in a Spad fighter, the crashing of a Gotha bomber into a barn, and a crash in a D7 Fokker. His preparations were meticulous and involved virtually rebuilding the Spad. The Spad crash, which occurred at more than 90 miles (145 km) per hour, was a complete success as was the barn crash. In the Fokker crash, however, Grace was not so lucky. Ideally a plane should crash on a wing tip so that the crumbling wing absorbs the impact, but in this case the plane landed on its nose. Grace's head went through the instrument panel and he suffered

serious neck injuries. Six weeks later, however, he discarded his plaster cast and was seen dancing in a San Antonio nightclub. He continued stunting and by the early 1930s estimated that he had survived 37 deliberate stunt crashes.

Various flying films followed *Wings*, one of the most notorious being *Hell's Angels* (1929). Directed by Howard Hughes, this film was extremely realistic but appallingly dangerous – four stuntmen were killed during the making of the film.

Flying films went out of vogue for a while, but from the 1950s Hollywood once more began to make use of aircraft. Since that time there have been a number of brilliant flying stunts. Two of the most notable are Paul Mantz's crash landing of a B17 for *Twelve O'Clock High* (1949) for which he was paid a record $6000, and Frank Tallman's spectacular stunt in *It's a Mad, Mad, Mad, Mad World* (1963) in which Tallman flew a two-engined Beechcraft straight through a billboard. Paul Mantz was later killed in a plane crash, at the age of 62, while filming *The Flight of the Phoenix* (1965). The film was dedicated to him

and, interestingly, was the first film to acknowledge the death of a stunt flier.

Cinema has also made spectacular use of the parachute as a stunting vehicle. Possibly one of the most brilliantly executed aerial stunts of recent years occurs in the opening sequence of *Moonraker* (1979). It is a skydiving sequence in which James Bond and a villainous pilot fight for a single parachute, the whole sequence taking place in free fall. As with all stunts, the action was carefully planned and tested, taking five weeks and 83 jumps to film. Three experienced skydivers doubled for the characters concerned, and specially designed 'suit parachutes' were worn that, in freefall, looked exactly like normal business suits.

In aviation, reckless barnstorming has today largely been replaced by the spectacular art of display flying. Teams such as the Red Arrows, Les Diables Rouges, and the Rothmans Aerobatic Team put on dazzling displays of aerobatics – specific high-precision manoeuvres that never fail to thrill a crowd.

The Rothmans Team, which normally consists of four or five members, uses Pitts Special biplanes for their display work. These aircraft are totally aerobatic and specially designed to fly as well upside-down as they do right side up. The team's manoeuvres include formation inside and outside loops, where the pilots hang in their straps, synchronised stall turns, the double mirror with two aircraft inverted above two flying erect, the leap-frog where two aircraft 'jump' over the other two, and their unique and extremely difficult slow roll in diamond formation.

Above: *A stuntman lowers himself down in a dangerous plane-to-plane transfer. Aerial stunts such as these enjoyed a terrific vogue in the 1920s and 1930s and attracted some of the most flamboyant and courageous personalities in the history of stunting. (Kobal Collection)*

Right: *British comedian Michael Crawford does his own sensational stunting for a television comedy series. (BBC Copyright)*

The art of display flying is extremely precise – it has to be, for as Rothmans' former team leader Bob Thompson has said '. . . if it's not, you hit the ground . . . or each other. . . ' The display takes considerable preparation and planning. Strangely enough, practice begins on the ground as the pilots walk through all the sequences, even the mirror manoeuvres for which the pilots turn round, face each other, and walk backwards. One of the main problems in display flying is disorientation and the trial walkthroughs help the pilots to fix the routines and aircraft positions firmly in their minds. Although most aerobatic pilots have a 'crib sheet' in the aircraft, it is very rarely used.

For an audience one of the most impressive manoeuvres is always the cross-over in which two or more aircraft cross each other's path apparently within a hair's breadth. In fact this manoeuvre is partly optical illusion. Pilot Mike Cairns describes the technique of the cross. 'We do the deep turning cross . . . and . . . also the flick, swivel and cross . . . What happens is that we always aim to cross each other left to left . . . that's part of the rules of the air; if you meet another aircraft coming head on, aircraft always turn to the right . . . so we stick to convention in this respect and ninety per cent of the time try to miss each other left to left . . . The technique adopted is that one pilot sets the line . . . he just flies a line . . . this is where the trust comes in between pilots, and the other pilot misses him. It doesn't matter if Bob for any reason can't see me; he will call "no contact" and we would both turn right, then almost certainly missing each other . . . I trust Bob so it doesn't matter how close it appears he is going to come to me, I just stay where I am, I never avoid him . . . The way we create the optical illusion to some point is we step ourselves in relation to the line of sight of the crowd, so that Bob may miss me by, say, 20 or 25 feet (6–8 m), and he will step himself up slightly higher so that from the crowd position these two aircraft do appear to be exactly level with each other . . . but one is slightly higher. We don't actually use depth to give ourselves separation though, we only use the miss distance.'

As Bob Thompson has summed up, 'What we

are trying to do is entertain people, and not really frighten them ... We're trying to get them excited ... but it's aimed at safety first.'

This same approach lies behind the performances of a unique team of aerial stunters, The Barnstormers Flying Circus. Formed in 1963 by Charles Boddington and Barry Tempest, the team, which describes itself as 'a rugby club that never grows up', consists of a number of highly competent pilots with considerable experience of flying light aircraft plus a number of experienced ground crew. The pilots operate on a part-time basis using various light aircraft such as the Tiger Moth, Chipmunk and Auster and their aim, as with the Rothmans team, is primarily to entertain rather than to frighten an audience. Inspired partly by the early air circuses, the team presents a variety of stunts ranging from stand-on-wing acts to mock battles, streamer cutting, balloon bursting, 'crazy' flying, limbo flying and solo aerobatics. The acts are presented very much in circus fashion with

plenty of colourful props, clowns, and fancy dress. But despite the light-hearted trimmings, the stunts rely on considerable skill and precision. As Barry Tempest has commented, in a show such as this 'the disciplines are very strong because it can be an extremely dangerous thing if the enthusiastic amateur is let loose on a crowd of people. An aeroplane, even a light aircraft, can do an awful lot of damage in the wrong place at the wrong time.'

All the stunts are carefully and precisely choreographed, worked out in meticulous detail. They have to be because although risks can be

Above: *A stunning display of aerobatics by the world-famous Red Arrows made even more spectacular by the use of smoke.* (*F D Trevarthen*)

Right: *The Rothmans Aerobatic Team in their Pitts Special bi-planes perform the double mirror manoeuvre in a display of high-precision aerobatics.* (*Rothmans*)

minimised they cannot be eliminated. All the acts require constant attention to detail and an instinctive feeling for the way in which the aircraft is standing up to the strains being put on it. In the Barnstormers' slightly unusual 'aerial omelette', fresh eggs are dropped from two aircraft travelling at around 60 knots (70 miles/ 113 km per hour) at heights of no more than 8 feet (2 m) above the ground. Remarkably, some 40 to 50 per cent of the eggs remain unbroken. In the limbo flying stunt, the aircraft fly even lower – as low as 2 or 3 inches (50–75 mm) above the ground. There is just no room for miscalculations.

Summing up what might be considered the philosophy behind such a form of entertainment, Barry Tempest has said 'the art of display flying, and it is an art, is very much making the easy look difficult, making the difficult look impossible, and leaving the impossible well alone.'

Left: *A collision seems inevitable as two aircraft perform an impressive cross-over. In fact this manoeuvre is partly optical illusion as there is more space between the aircraft than it would appear from the ground.* (F D Trevarthen)

Right: *A stand-on-wing display by the British Barnstormers Flying Circus. The stuntwoman is strapped to a rig bolted on top of a Tiger Moth aircraft. The pilot also has to be skilful since the aircraft is subject to considerable increase in drag.* (F D Trevarthen)

Left: 'Colonel Crackshot', a low-altitude stand-on-wing act in which the 'passenger' shoots at a target of balloons surrounding a spread-eagled figure. (F D Trevarthen)

Below: A shot from Superman (1978). The flying sequences in Superman were achieved by the use of wires which were attached to extremely uncomfortable harnesses worn by the stunt people. (Kobal Collection)

Combat Stunting

The origins of modern stage and screen fights go back a long way; in fact combat as a form of entertainment has a very long history. In the ancient world it probably reached its most spectacular form in the gladiatorial contests of ancient Rome.

From about 264 BC until they were finally outlawed in about AD 404, contests between professional fighters or gladiators were a highly popular form of entertainment throughout the Roman Empire. Vast audiences flocked to the contests which were held in specially built arenas some of which could accommodate as many as 20 000 spectators. The gladiators were paired off to fight with each other, usually to the number of about 100 couples, although in the days of Augustus massive gladiatorial displays were given involving as many as 10 000 gladiators.

The gladiators themselves were highly trained and skilled fighters, originally coming from the ranks of slaves or prisoners but later professionals in their own right. Contests were usually to the death, the fate of the defeated gladiator often being decided by the crowd. The essence of the entertainment was its brutality and in this respect it differs from modern combat entertainment in which the emphasis is definitely on safety.

By the Middle Ages the tournament and associated single-combat jousting had become extremely exciting forms of public spectacle. Based on the ideas of chivalry, tournaments became the occasion for considerable pageantry and displays of skill. Like the earlier gladiatorial contests from which they may have descended, medieval jousts were extremely dangerous and many knights were killed or injured. Even today modern jousting carries a high degree of risk.

The travelling fairs of medieval Europe featured displays of sword fighting and fencing and by the time of Elizabeth I, public displays of swordsmanship drew large crowds. Dramatic combat sequences were incorporated into the plays of the time, particularly those of Shakespeare. Being accustomed to public duelling, theatre audiences were probably highly critical of stage fights and those in *Hamlet* or *Macbeth* for example were of a very high standard. Richard Tarlton, one of the great Elizabethan actors, was himself a first-class fencer.

Very few actors today are experienced swordsmen, but stage fights are still spectacular and demand a high degree of skill. Often a fight is the dramatic climax of a play and it must look both exciting and authentic to maintain the play's momentum and the interest of the audience. To make a stage fight look effective,

Left: *A stained glass window in Chartres Cathedral, France, depicts a 13th century jousting scene. In medieval Europe, jousting was one of the most exciting forms of public spectacle.* *(Ronald Sheridan)*

Above: *Douglas Fairbanks Senior escapes injury by sliding down the bannisters in a classic sequence from* The Three Musketeers *(1921). (Kobal Collection)*

and at the same time to ensure safety, takes considerable planning, and this is the responsibility of the fight arranger.

Planning a fight takes a great deal of skill; it has even been described as an art. Like choreographing a ballet or dance routine, the fight arranger establishes the overall pattern of the fight, taking into account such things as scenery and other actors on the stage, and then works out each individual move. By paying attention to pauses, body and sword patterns, and to differing rhythms in a fight, even a short routine can be extremely effective.

Once the routine has been established and the actors' confidence built up, rehearsals are essential. Sword fights are complex and difficult for someone without practical experience. If a sword, even a specially prepared sword, is swung about haphazardly it can be very dangerous. The aim of the rehearsals is to minimise risks. Footwork in particular is carefully worked out and rehearsed as it is the basis of a safe fight.

Actors, having first been trained in sword work, then have to memorise the fight sequence in precise detail. It is worth remembering that by the time the actors have to fight they may well have been on stage for two hours, and a fight sequence that may last a few minutes can be gruelling. That same sequence will also have to be repeated night after night, a real test of stamina.

But spectacular as theatre fights are, they are restricted by the very nature of theatre. The same does not apply to cinema which suffers from none of the physical limitations imposed by a stage. The choice of locations and sets, the

61

use of sound effects and dubbing, plus the use of specialist stuntmen as doubles, have led to spectacular screen fights that just could not have been produced on a stage.

Another advantage that cinema has over the stage is that an actor rarely has to either memorise a long complex sequence, or even to fight very much at all. Fights are usually filmed in a series of short scenes, the whole being put together at a later stage by the editor. Stuntmen normally double the main actors for the 'master shot' in which the entire sequence is filmed, and shots of the principals are inserted or 'cut in' to the master shot where appropriate.

As in the theatre, however, the success of a screen fight largely depends on the work of a fight arranger. The first specialist fight arranger used in the cinema was Belgian fencing master Henry Uyttenhove who was called in to supervise the sword play in *The Mark of Zorro* (1920) which featured Douglas Fairbanks Senior. Fairbanks was the first star to regularly use fencing in his films although he tended to use weapons as props for his remarkable stunts rather than for well-executed swordplay.

Swashbuckling films remained highly popular throughout the 1920s, and as the demand for more authentic and complex swordplay increased, the fight arranger became, and has remained, a vital component. Uyttenhove went on to supervise a number of fight sequences including those in *The Three Musketeers* (1921), *The Prisoner of Zenda* (1922) and *Scaramouche* (1923).

Another Belgian fencing master, Fred Cavens, was also an important duel arranger and became permanent fencing coach to Douglas Fairbanks. Cavens not only arranged duels in such films as *The Black Pirate* (1926) and *Captain Blood* (1935) but also doubled for many of the stars. Cavens was largely responsible for establishing the style of the screen fight. Strange as it may seem, competition fighting rarely looks effective on the screen; the finer points are completely missed

Left: *Gene Kelly, playing the part of D'Artagnan, leaps for the chandelier in an exciting scene from the 1948 version of* The Three Musketeers. *(Kobal Collection)*

by an audience and it can look quite dull. For film the strokes have to be slowed down to some extent and exaggerated but at the same time complete authenticity must be maintained.

The 1940s saw a revival of interest in historical and costume films and many of the earlier films were remade. By this time sword fights had become highly skilled and the period produced some of the most memorable duels in the history of cinema. A classic fight designed by Ralph Faulkener occurs in *The Prisoner of Zenda* (1937) between Ronald Coleman and Douglas Fairbanks Junior, and another in *The Three Musketeers* (1948) in which dancer Gene Kelly performs a brilliantly executed sword routine lasting five minutes, which was then a record. A third spectacular sword fight is that between Mel Ferrer and Stewart Granger in *Scaramouche* (1952) which lasts a full six and a half minutes.

The swashbuckling movies were hard work and demanded a high degree of skill. They also had their dangers. Douglas Fairbanks Junior has mentioned that he nearly took someone's

Above: *The sword fight between Stewart Granger and Mel Ferrer in* Scaramouche *(1952) lasted six and a half minutes and has rightly become one of the classic examples of cinema swordplay.* (*Kobal Collection*)

eye out in a duel, and this with a blunted sword. And likewise actor Cornel Wilde nearly lost a finger when a real scimitar was used in a rehearsal instead of a dulled one.

It is precisely because of injuries such as these, or worse, that a well-prepared fight routine is essential. And it has to be adhered to; an enthusiastic amateur either forgetting or breaking away from the set routine can cause mayhem.

It has been said that a fight routine is one of the most difficult stunts to produce – it has to look as realistic as possible but it never actually can be. The standard punch-up or brawl so popular in Westerns is a prime example. It is a highly stylised form of fighting, specially designed for the screen and largely developed by John Wayne and stuntman Yakima Canutt.

63

Obviously two men punching each other on the screen cannot use real punches; instead they use exaggerated motions and fake the punches. A successful result depends on the stuntman's acting abilities and the positioning of the camera. Depending on where the camera is placed, a punch to the head may miss by up to 6 inches (150 mm). The person throwing the punch makes a great show of doing so; in turn the person receiving the punch must jerk his head back or to the side fast and in such a way that it looks as if he has received a hard punch on the jaw. Punches to various other parts of the body such as the stomach or shoulders may connect although they too can be faked in much the same way. If they do connect the punches must be 'pulled' and the person receiving the punch will wear padding.

The same Western-style bar-room brawl often contains a shot of a chair or bottle being broken over an opponent's head, or a stumble back onto a table that then collapses. Props such as these are the responsibility of the special effects depart-

Above: A punch-up in the traditional Western style from Thunder in God's Country. *Frequently very effective, this is a highly stylised form of fighting in which actual bodily contact is rarely made. (Kobal Collection)*

ment. The fight arranger or co-ordinator is responsible for the way in which they are incorporated into the fight.

Chairs, tables, and other furniture used in a fight are usually made of balsa wood, scored so that it disintegrates on impact. Hit by such props, a stuntman may be bruised but should not be injured. Of course the unexpected can happen – a flying chip of balsa wood has been known to break a stuntman's nose.

All the weapons used in a fight are faked in some way. Knives can be made of rubber but more frequently are plastic. Wounds are also a matter of artifice and can be produced in various ways. A wound can be applied to the actor by the make-up staff before the scene is shot.

While filming takes place, the actor masks his wound from the camera by positioning his body in a certain way. As he is apparently slashed by the knife, the actor turns quickly thereby displaying the wound. Alternatively 'blood' can be squirted through tubes running through the handle of the knife into the blade. Small quantities of synthetic blood can be stored in the handle of the knife which is then squeezed or, if larger quantities are needed, they can be pumped through a tube hidden under the actor's clothing and connected to the knife. This particular method was used in the dramatic throat-cutting sequence in *The Wild Bunch* (1969).

Fights with spears and bows and arrows are usually performed by specialists who work in close collaboration with the special effects department. The impression of an arrow piercing someone is achieved in various ways. Often an arrow is fired by compressed air along a thin wire which runs through the whole length of the arrow, one end of the wire being attached to the stuntman who wears a cork- or balsa-covered metal plate. Underneath this he also wears padding.

A snap-up arrow can also be used, particularly for these scenes in which an unsuspecting victim is hit by an unseen enemy. The snap-up arrow lies vertically under the actor's clothing, shaft down. The arrow is released by a spring mechanism so that the shaft pops up straight giving the impression that the arrow has just been driven into the victim's body.

Right: *A stuntman slides to the ground pierced by arrows in the chest and arm. There are a number of ways of producing arrow hits. Usually a specialist archer is used. The arrows may be fired directly at the stuntman who is protected by padding and balsa wood worn under his clothing. Alternatively arrows may be fired by compressed air along a thin wire. (Kobal Collection)*

Page 66: *An actor staggers backwards as a result of gunshot wounds. In the films of the 1960s and 1970s combat sequences became increasingly realistic. (Kobal Collection)*

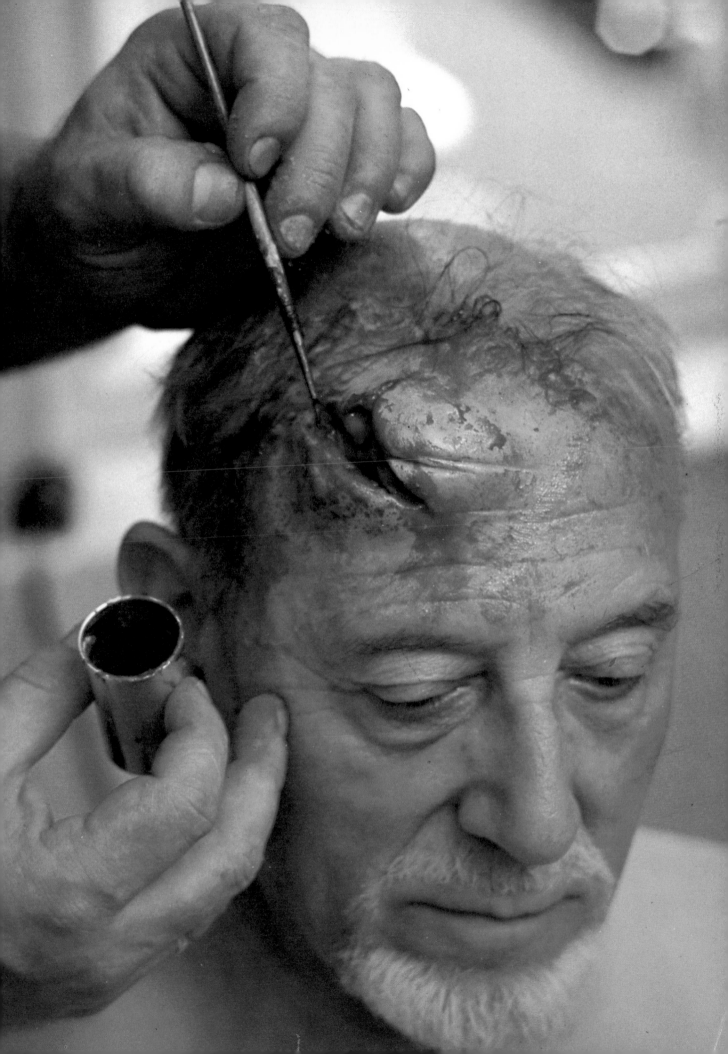

The close-up effect of a knife, arrow or spear actually entering a body usually involves the use of a dummy torso. This shot is then quickly followed by one of the actor with the weapon realistically fitted in place.

Dramatic and in some cases horrific effects have been produced to show the results of people hit by bullets. Normally so-called 'squibs' are used. First introduced in the 1930s, squibs are tiny, smokeless, explosive charges mounted on thin metal plates and detonated electrically. They can be detonated by small batteries strapped to the actors or by being attached to a control board. They can even be detonated by radio control. Often a thin rubber sac, usually a condom, is filled with synthetic blood and taped over the squib for greater realism. The squib explodes outwards in a remarkably realistic fashion without causing any injury to the actors.

Probably some of the most spectacular examples of mass bullet hits occur in *The Wild Bunch* (1969) and in *Bonnie and Clyde* (1968). For the final death scene in *Bonnie and Clyde*, literally hundreds of squibs were used, and hours were spent creating the overall effect. In order to produce the effect of bullets passing through the car into Faye Dunaway's body the sequence was filmed in a number of takes, in each one exactly corresponding squibs were detonated both on the car body and on Faye Dunaway's body.

Page 67: *A highly realistic head wound is painted onto an actor by a member of the make-up department. In Britain this type of synthetic blood is known as Kensington Gore.* (*Daily Telegraph Colour Library*)

Page 70: *A brawl in outer space – one of the action sequences from* Moonraker *(1979), the latest James Bond movie.* (*United Artists*)

Right: *One of the final sequences from* The Wild Bunch. *The effects of bullet hits are produced by 'squibs', tiny explosive charges placed on the actor's body, that explode outwards in a very effective way.* (*Kobal Collection*)

Below: *A scene of total devastation from* The Wild Bunch *(1969). It was films such as* The Wild Bunch *and* Bonnie and Clyde *(1968) that set the trend for realistic violence in films.* (*Kobal Collection*)

Introducing Animals

Stunting with animals and in particular horses goes back a long way. Most modern circus and cinema horse work is based on a tradition that stretches back certainly as far as Ancient Rome and probably also Ancient Greece. In the arenas of Ancient Rome, trick riding together with chariot racing was a popular spectacle. Riders leaped from one galloping horse to another, performed various horseback acrobatics and hung from their horses to pick up objects from the ground.

By the 1700s, horsemanship had become a very impressive form of entertainment. In England Thomas Johnson, the Irish Tartar, was renowned for his display of Roman Riding in which he stood on two running horses with a third moving horse sandwiched in between. So popular was this type of trick riding that it is still performed today.

Another horseman, Daniel Wildman, introduced a unique spectacle – trick riding with a swarm of bees covering his head – a stunt which probably has not been repeated. And Philip Astley, often called the father of the modern circus, also performed remarkable tricks like standing one-legged on horseback with the other foot in his mouth while his horse jumped a fence. It was Astley, also, who invented the circus ring, having discovered that it was easier to balance on a moving horse as it travelled in a circle.

Astley's successor, Andrew Ducrow, was probably one of the greatest of these early equestrians. He perfected a lavish act of daring known as 'The Courier of St Petersburg' which remained popular throughout the 1800s. It consisted of a rider standing astride two galloping horses while other horses went between his legs. To add colour to the display, the horses bore the flags of those countries a courier would pass through en route to St Petersburg.

Somersaults are the basis of a trick rider's repertoire – the first recorded backward somersault on a moving horse being performed in 1839. James Robinson, a great successor of the Astleys and Ducrows, actually performed twenty-three consecutive somersaults, alternating backward and forward. In more recent times it is the Cristianis who hold the distinction of being the best-known circus trick riders. They have been called 'the somersaulters supreme'. Their connection with the circus goes back to the mid-1800s and by the early 1900s they had their own circus. Their speciality 'suicide trick' consists of three members of the family standing on the backs of three moving horses, one in front of the other. Simultaneously the three perform a backward somersault through hoops, the last man in

Above left: *Bull-leaping from an Ancient Cretan fresco some 4000 years ago. This ancient and dangerous stunt involved somersaulting over the back of a moving bull and could be considered the ancestor of some of the modern trick-riding acts performed today.* (Robert Harding Associates)

Below left: *Trick riders training at a circus school. The art and skill of trick riding has a long tradition in the history of entertainment.* (Daily Telegraph Colour Library)

Above: *A rodeo rider in Alberta, Canada, pits his wits against the frantic movements of a bucking horse. Many professional horse stuntmen went into cinema from the rodeo.* (Robert Estall, R Vroom)

the line landing on the ground. Lucio Cristiani surpassed even this by doing a back somersault from one running horse, passing over a second, and landing on a third.

In 1845 Laurent Franconi, son of the Venetian circus master Antoine Franconi, introduced Roman chariot races in Paris. Chariot racing came back into fashion for a while but was soon eclipsed by the Wild West Show created by Buffalo Bill Cody. Buffalo Bill's show featured non-stop action and riding skills still seen in modern rodeo today. The United States had its own tradition of trick riding, based largely on the mythology of the Wild West. It was from this background of the professional cowboy and rodeo rider that horse stuntmen for the early Hollywood Westerns began to emerge. Some became stars in their own right. Tom Mix was one of these. There are many colourful stories about this man who, everyone agreed, had 'guts and more to spare'. By the time he died in 1940 at the age of 60, both the bones of his arm and shoulder were held together with surgical wire and his body was a scarred wreck.

Many well-known actors have done their own horse stunts. Gary Cooper actually began his film career as a stunt rider and John Wayne also did the occasional horse stunt, as a journalist in

the 1958 version of *Ben Hur*. On the whole, however, the great stunt riders of the Westerns are names that the public has never heard of. They include stuntman Cliff Lyons who performed an astounding 60 to 70 foot (18–21 m) leap on horseback from the edge of a cliff into water, and the great Yakima Canutt.

Canutt became a legend in his own time because it was he who specialised in expanding and improving stunt riding techniques, taking cowboy or rodeo skills and adapting them for the cinema. One example was 'bulldogging'. In rodeo this consists of catching a calf from horseback, getting it to the ground and tying its feet. It was a stunt custom-made for cinema and could fairly easily be adapted to a situation where another man replaces the calf. In an interview Canutt described the development of the stunt which has become a feature of the Western. 'You did bulldogging: you take a man off a horse by grabbing him, fall between the horses, and get run over half the time. Well, I built up to where you jump light on the horse and go on over with the man, and then I got to where I could make it in one jump. It became a much more spectacular deal, and safer, because you cleared the horses.'

Canutt was particularly skilled at the transfer – the classic Western stunt of transferring from a galloping horse to a moving object such as a stagecoach. Probably the most dramatic example of this transfer occurs in *Stagecoach* (1939). It contains a spectacular scene where an Indian, played by Canutt, transfers from his horse onto the lead horse of a stagecoach team. He takes the reins but is shot by the driver so then falls to the 'tongue' between the horses and, after dragging along the ground for a moment, lets go. The coach and horses then speed over him. So that the horses would not change direction and pull the coach over him, Canutt had to have the horses moving fast and commented 'I found I could drop off as fast as 50 miles (80 km) an hour, and as long as I was relaxed from the belt down I wouldn't roll.' Not only did Canutt do that sequence but also doubled for John Wayne, a passenger who saves the runaway coach by climbing along to the lead horses, taking the reins and pulling it to a stop.

Above: *'Bulldogging' in a scene from* Duel at Diablo *(1966). This particular stunt has become a standard feature of the Western and is a perfect example of a rodeo skill that was deliberately adapted for cinema stunting.* (Kobal Collection)

Left: *A stuntman tackles a charging bull in a dramatic shot from* J W Coop *(1972), a shot that demonstrates the sort of risks that are part of a stuntman's everyday work.* (Kobal Collection)

the late 1920s recalled: 'Duke took a running jump on a horse and rode like the wind, rolling under the saddle and hanging beneath the horse's belly. As the speeding horse neared Yates (head of the Republic Studios) Duke rolled completely off with a perfectly executed fall – just like the stuntmen do . . . He got up, dusted off his cowboy clothes and walked over to Yates. "Let's see your Roy Rogers do that, Herb".'

Charlton Heston also did his own horsefalls in

This sort of transfer work is still being done today. It is always a dangerous stunt and relies on careful preparation and precise timing. British stuntwoman Sue Crosland describes a transfer from a horse to a moving train that she filmed in Spain: 'We built up from about 20 miles per hour to about 30 miles per hour (32–48 km.p.h). We were going some. I rehearsed in as much as I galloped up and down with the horse to get the timing of the speed of the train and my speed, and where I wanted to actually do the transfer . . . The train's got to go in time with the horse – you can't be expecting to push a horse on too much . . . it's just so difficult with horses.'

The most commonly performed stunt in modern horse work is the horse fall. In the earliest days of the Westerns it was acceptable for a man to either pull up his horse and then fall off, or, as stunting techniques improved, to fall directly off a moving horse which then carried on riderless. But as action became more spectacular it was necessary that the horse itself be brought down. Initially two methods were widely used – the 'pit' fall and the 'running W.'

For the pit fall a trench was dug in the ground, filled with cardboard boxes as cushioning, and then covered. At the far end of the pit was a slope. The unsuspecting horse galloped into the pit and, once it had recovered from the shock, scrambled out up the slope. If the horse could not get out, it panicked, as stuntman Jack Cooper discovered when a horse in difficulty kicked out wildly at him.

The running W method of bringing down a horse was an adaptation of an old cowboy method of breaking horses. Types of running W vary but essentially it consisted of a cable staked to the ground which was passed through a ring under the horse's belly, down to a hobble on one front leg, up again and then down to the other front leg, forming a W shape. When taut, the cable pulled the horse's legs up and produced an effective fall.

In the 1930s there was much public outcry about these two techniques, and although Canutt claimed that he had done more than 300 running Ws without mishap, even he had to admit a badly-planned one could be brutal. B Reeves 'Breezy' Eason directed the dramatic charge in the 1936 version of *The Charge of the Light Brigade* – probably the most notable example of mass horsefalls in cinema – and although himself an excellent horseman, gained a reputation of being ruthless in his quest for realism. In this particular film thirty horses were killed and two hundred and forty stuntmen were injured! According to a witness of the filming, a special pit was dug for the bodies of the injured animals.

In 1940 both methods were banned by the American Humane Society, although the running W is still used in some countries today. As a result it became necessary to train horses specifically for stunting. Today only trained horses tend to be used in the cinema. Training takes time and patience. As stuntman Hal Needham pointed out 'Training a horse to fall on cue is, I think, the most difficult horse stunt there is, because it's so much against his nature.' Training a horse can take anything up to a year, and it may take much longer to get a really good falling horse. To start with, the horse learns to fall on a lunge rope, one foreleg bent and tied up with a rope attached to a pulley. Gradually the horse learns that every time his head is pulled round, he has to fall and the rope is removed from his leg. Eventually the horse will fall naturally 'on the bit'.

Working with horses needs careful preparation and it is vital that the right kind of horses are used. Sue Crosland has commented that 'You can't just go out and get a horse from a riding school and expect it to do the sort of things that you want it to. . . .' Describing a reinactment of Boadicea in which about fifty untrained and even unshod horses were used, she said that 'as soon as they saw a shield or a spear or a sword

Two horses and a buckboard leap from a cliff in a shot from Phantom Rider *(1937). This stunt was usually achieved by tipping terrified horses down a greased chute; in this particular example the horses are also wearing blinkers. It was a very dangerous and inhumane stunt and has since been banned by the American Humane Society. (John Topham Picture Library)*

UN DOMPTEUR BLESSÉ PAR UN LION

and you tried to get close enough up to somebody else to actually have a battle . . . they were frightened out of their minds. We persevered for a bit, but I think we all came off at least once because they just went straight up in the air and dumped you on the ground.'

A stuntman taking a fall aims to land on ground that has been prepared – perhaps ploughed and covered with peat. He may also use special 'falling' stirrups and wear padding.

Above: *A stuntman is dragged along the ground behind a galloping horse. As shown here, for this stunt the stuntman is wired to the stirrup of the horse, the other end of the wire being attached to the stuntman's jacket. In horse work this is possibly one of the most dangerous types of fall. The horse is trained not to kick out at the actor but there is always the risk of an accident.* (Kobal Collection)

Left: *This turn of the century illustration of a lion tamer being mauled by a lion clearly shows the dangers of working with wild animals.* (Mansell Collection)

'Jerk' harnesses that snatch the stuntman out of the saddle can also be used. But horse falls are always hard work and can be extremely dangerous; it has been said that horse work is second only to aerial stunting in danger. In 1959 stuntman Fred Kennedy was killed doing quite a simple horse fall for *The Horse Soldiers* (1959). And there are other risks too. Costume may create an unforeseen hazard. If a shoe, for example, gets stuck in the stirrup, a stuntman may miss the prepared ground and land some feet away on whatever the surface may be. Above all, as Sue Crosland has said, 'in horse work . . . it's a matter of rehearsing and rehearsing, but only to a certain point, because animals get very bored very quickly . . . It's not like getting in a car . . . you know what a car is capable of, and if the brakes are good and the rest of it. But you get on a horse and it can take anything into its

head. It's like working with animals period. They really are very unpredictable creatures.'

Obviously horses are not the only animals that have been used in stunting. Bears, lions, dogs, elephants, alligators and even rats are just a few other examples. It has been said that 'for cinema thrills, the wild animal has no equal'. Pioneer film producers preferred fakes, but as audiences grew more discerning stuffed tigers and men dressed in gorilla suits were replaced by live wild animals.

The risks to the stuntmen were often appalling. In one interview stuntman Joe Bonomo described a sequence from *The Sign of the Cross* (1932) in which he played a Christian slave thrown into a pit of alligators, his only protection being five men ready to push poles into the alligators' mouths if necessary. 'We waited until my particular alligator was a little apart from the rest, then two husky Roman soldiers threw me in beside him. As I hit the mud I grabbed him by the front leg . . . We wrestled for a moment, and he opened his big lower jaw. I grabbed it with my left hand, held it open,

Below: *Two alligators are pulled into water in readiness for filming. Despite the unpredictability of wild animals, an entire range of different creatures have been used in the cinema.* (*Kobal Collection*)

half put my head in his mouth, but from the side away from the cameras. From the camera side it looked as though my head was in his mouth. Then I slammed it shut and held it shut . . . I quickly pulled him down on top of me, kicking my legs violently just once, then stiffened them out suddenly . . . slowly relaxed and fell "lifeless".'

Above: A carefully-planned sequence from an early Safari movie. Hardly surprisingly, the actor on the ground looks genuinely terrified. (Kobal Collection)

Page 81: Snake charming has been practised in India and other Eastern countries since the very earliest times. Generally a cobra is used and the reptile's fangs are removed. (Mansell Collection)

Right: In this colourful illustration a snake charmer finds herself in difficulties when she is attacked by one of her boas. (Mansell Collection)

CHARMEUSE DE SERPENTS ATTAQUÉE PAR UN BOA

Such a stunt could only have been performed by a real professional. Tom Mix showed the same amazing coolness in the making of the serial *Lost in the Jungle* (1914). A leopard jumped on the leading actress and he pulled it off by the tail. Directors were often far from sympathetic to the risks these early stuntmen were taking. Cecil B de Mille insisted that Bonomo and the alligators were sprayed with oil to make them gleam dramatically, making Bonomo's task of wrestling with them much more perilous.

In *Darkest Africa* (1936) 'Breezy' Eason dismissed experienced animal-handler Clyde Beatty's objections to wrestling bare-handed with a tiger in a pit. The animal went wild and Beatty had to be saved by attendants, who rattled the tiger's cage door, an old trick that often works because animals associate it with food. As the badly-shaken and bleeding Beatty emerged, Eason said excitedly: 'Boy, that was swell! Get your breath, Clyde, and we'll do a re-take. . . .'

Making the Impossible Possible

Illusion and stunting are quite closely linked – to some extent both create fantasy worlds where the impossible is realised. In the history of entertainment, illusionists, conjurers, and magicians have attracted a large and credulous following for thousands of years. Their basic appeal is mystery; illusionists rely on the secrecy surrounding their skills and techniques and it is a secrecy that is jealously guarded. Common to all illusionists is the ability to deceive but it is a highly technical and skilled ability and a perfectly legitimate one.

The art of conjuring goes back to the time when the belief in magic was universal. It was practised some 5000 years ago by the ancient Egyptians and subsequently by the Greeks and Romans. In eastern countries it has flourished likewise for thousands of years. By the middle ages, in Europe, conjurers and magicians had become as common a feature of street entertainment and travelling fairs as acrobats and jugglers. One of the best-known conjurers in the 18th century was Isaac Fawkes who had booths at all the British fairs. One of his most puzzling feats was to cause an apple tree to blossom and fruit within less than a minute. On his death in 1731, Fawkes left an estate of £10 000, an almost unheard of sum in those days.

Sword-swallowers, fire-eaters and other illusionists were all closely associated with the travelling fair before they became part of either the circus or the music hall. Sword-swallowing is an ancient art that is said to be fairly simple once the natural urge to gag has been overcome. Performers at various times have swallowed, and regurgitated, not only swords but also various other objects including ivory balls, watches, goldfish, frogs and even live rats.

Fire-eating too is an ancient skill. Originating in India, it takes many forms, all of them impressive. Fire-eaters can, and have, put virtually any blazing materials into their mouths provided they remember to breathe out so that the heat is kept away from the mouth; the wetted tongue and mouth provide insulation against the fire. Nevertheless there have been accidents and even fatalities. In India and elsewhere, specially-prepared hemp has been used for fire tricks. It is put into the mouth glowing and bursts into flames only when air is expelled through the mouth. In the 18th century Robert Powell was one of the most renowned British fire-eaters. His act included eating red-hot coals, licking red-hot tobacco pipes and, as the culmination of his act, sipping a mixture of melted wax, alum, lead, resin, and pitch – a mixture fondly known as 'his dish of soup'.

Another mystifying but highly dangerous trick

is bullet-catching. Possibly first introduced in the early 17th century, it has caused the death of many illusionists, usually because someone has replaced the rigged bullets or weapons with real ones. In the past, guns with blocked-up barrels were used and bullets were made of wax or soap covered with graphite. Today, with the skepticism of modern audiences, it has become harder to rig this act but it still continues to be performed with great success.

Many of the more remarkable illusions stem from the East, and India in particular. One of the best known is the extraordinary Indian Rope Trick in which a conjurer sits cross-legged on the ground and throws one end of a rope into the air. The rope stiffens and stands up on end rather like a pole. It is then climbed by a small boy who vanishes into thin air. Probably one of the most famous illusions in the world, and crudely imitated on many occasions, it still remains an unsolved mystery. Another traditionally Indian illusion is that of the boy and the basket. For this a boy steps into a basket which is then closed. The illusionist stabs the basket several times with a long knife, the stabbing being accompanied by realistic screams and much 'blood'. The boy subsequently steps out quite unharmed, having been protected by the construction of the basket which allows him to lie around the sides and so avoid the knife thrusts. In some versions the boy disappears completely, usually into a cavity underneath.

The age of the great modern illusionists began in the 19th century with the age of science. One of the earliest illusionists of that era was the remarkable Frenchman Jean-Eugene Robert-Houdin. From the 1830s until his death in 1871 he fascinated audiences with his displays of 'levitation' in which objects and even people were suspended in the air by means of concealed rods. Another great illusionist was Sir John Nevil Maskelyne. Working with a partner George A Cooke, and subsequently with David

As this illustration shows, the ancinet art of fire-eating is still a popular feature of outdoor entertainment. (Daily Telegraph Colour Library, Michael Hardy)

83

Devant, he performed at the Egyptian Hall, Piccadilly, London for more than thirty years. Among other illusions, Maskelyne and Devant perfected the levitation trick in which an assistant is suspended in the air and a hoop passed around his body from all directions. Maskelyne also invented a wooden cabinet in which disappearing tricks were performed, and a trick box from which he could perform various escapes.

Other illusionists of the time included Monsieur de Kolta, inventor of the famous Vanishing Lady trick, and P T Selbit who in 1920 originated the 'Sawing a Woman in Two' act, later expanded and popularised by the Polish-born magician, Horace Goldin.

But foremost of all the illusionists of that time was undoubtedly the great Harry Houdini. He was born Erik Weisz in Budapest in 1874 but adopted the name Houdini, after Robert-Houdin, shortly after he began his career in 1891. Until his break came in 1899, Houdini worked mainly in small town shows in the United States, often dangerously near to poverty. On one occasion he shared the bill with Joe and Myra Keaton, a married couple specialising in songs and comic routines. Their son, Joseph, was part of their knock-about comedy team and because of his tendency to bash into things and remain unscathed, Houdini nicknamed him 'Buster', a name that was to become a household word during the days of the silent movies.

From 1899 until his death in 1926 Houdini rose to be the undisputed, though not necessarily unchallenged, king of escapology. He made escapology an art, freeing himself from ropes, straitjackets, handcuffs, and all manner of bonds

Left: *The famous Indian rope trick, probably one of the oldest illusions of all, and still not satisfactorily explained.* (*Mary Evans Picture Library*)

Right: *The great Harry Houdini shown here as quite a young man. Even today Houdini is still regarded as the greatest escapologist of all.* (*Mary Evans Picture Library*)

Above left: *A famous shot from* King Kong *(1933), a film that used virtually every special effects technique known at the time, and one that has become a classic of its kind.* *(Kobal Collection)*

Below left: *The aftermath of a stunt – a film set created to show the effects of a bomb explosion in a London street. The 'bomb crater' is a 10 ft (3 m) deep hole, dug out and then blasted with dynamite packed in steel drums. Stuntmen, playing the part of Londoners injured by the explosion, lie on the ground waiting for close-up shots.* *(Kobal Collection)*

Above right: *An action sequence such as this one from* The Green Berets *(1968) demands meticulous planning and split-second timing to avoid injury. Despite the realism of this particular scene, no-one was injured.* *(Kobal Collection)*

in all manner of situations. He said himself that nothing could hold him, not even jails, and among his other exploits he effected an escape from a steel-lined Siberian prison van and a top-security Washington jail. A favourite trick of his was to escape from a padlocked can filled with water and from 1908 to 1912 it was a permanent feature of his vaudeville act.

More than fifty years after his death people are still puzzled by how Houdini achieved his successes. Physically he was both agile and extremely skilful; he could hold his breath for three minutes and could even untie simple knots or fastenings with his toes. Probably, too, he made use of the age-old methods of flexing his muscles or expanding his chest as his bonds were being fastened making it easier to wriggle free later. It is also likely that some of his stunts were rigged. It is said that he used duplicate ropes, and that he had keys and knives secreted about his body or even in the various cabinets and boxes into which he was placed. The cabinets and boxes themselves may also have been rigged, but we'll never know.

However, regardless of the tricks he may have employed, many of Houdini's stunts were extremely dangerous and his achievements took courage and skill. He remained alive because he knew and worked within his limits, never taking unnecessary risks and always meticulously planning his stunts – precepts which he advised barnstormer and stuntman Ormer Locklear to follow. Above all, Houdini was a remarkable performer and showman, a pastmaster at exciting an audience. Never one to make a stunt look too easy, it is said that having already made his escape he would wait for as long as twenty minutes before showing himself to the audience in order to get the maximum effect.

Houdini's achievements gave rise to a number of legends even during his lifetime. One concerned an aerial stunt that he was supposed to have performed in 1919. He had already featured in a fairly successful film serial *The Master Mystery* (1919) and in 1919 went on to work on a full-length feature film *The Grim Game*. Action in this called for Houdini to perform a dramatic mid-air plane-to-plane transfer. When the scene was shot the aircraft collided, became entangled and spiralled earthwards, finally coming apart some 200 feet (61 m) above the ground. Miraculously no-one was hurt and actual footage of the accident was kept and used in the film. One of

Houdini's best-kept secrets at the time was that in fact he was nowhere near the plane but had been doubled by an ex-flier and stuntman Robert E Kennedy. However, no-one came forward to prove it.

In the cinema the role of illusionist falls to the people in the special effects department. Their job involves inventiveness and skill and covers an almost indefinable range. At one end of the scale it is the special effects department that creates the illusion of a man walking up a wall or of a giant gorilla rampaging through New York City; at the other end of the scale it is the special effects department that is responsible for adding realism to stunt action, for working out ways or means of achieving almost impossible situations while at the same time minimising dangers.

To a great extent it was the development of special effects combined with the skills and courage of stuntmen that opened up the possibilities for really spectacular stunting. High falls are a case in point – increasingly dramatic falls have only been possible with the development of the box rig since the 1930s. The same applies to breakaway objects such as chairs and glass. The first breakaway windows were made of sugar boiled into toffee to produce the so-called toffee glass. On film it looked just like glass and shattered in much the same way but without the dangers. However toffee glass did have a disadvantage – under the hot lights of the studio it tended to melt and as a result was replaced by resin. Today glass and most other breakaway objects are made from plastics such as polyurethane and styrofoam.

As with stunting in general, many special effects ideas were born in the 1920s and 1930s. One was the studio tank used for filming scenes with water, either with full-scale sets or with miniatures. Although ideally not more than 3 feet (1 m) deep, the tanks were large; MGM for example had a 300-foot (91-m) square tank. Working in the tank was often uncomfortable but usually safe; when dump tanks were used as well, however, it could become dangerous. Essentially dump tanks were special tanks built either above the main tank or onto its side. They were used to release an enormous amount of

Above left: British stuntman Terry Walsh, enveloped in flames, runs out of a burning building and down the street as part of the action in a television series. Fire gags such as these are probably the most dangerous stunts of all. (BBC Copyright)

Far left: Two stuntmen, one covered in flames, prepare for a rooftop fight in a Universal Studios production. The appearance of the oncoming stuntman gives some idea of the protective clothing worn for a fire gag. (Ronald Grant)

Near left: British stuntman Jack Cooper emerges from a terrifying blaze that nearly cost him his life. Before the stunt a routine had been carefully planned involving two explosions; unpredictably three explosions actually occurred. (Jack Cooper)

water – sometimes several thousand gallons – in a very short space of time. Filming *Noah's Ark* (1929) some 600 000 gallons (2 724 000 litres) of water were unleashed onto extras. Many people were seriously injured and three were killed. Since that time however, stringent safety regulations have prevented similar incidents, and terrific effects have been produced including the sequence in *Tora! Tora! Tora!* (1970) where the Japanese fleet battles its way through a storm to Pearl Harbour. For this particular sequence miniatures were used.

During the 1960s and 1970s the accent on violence in the cinema has kept special effects busy producing more and more gore. Whether it is always necessary to show graphically the effects of violence is debatable; in Hitchcock's *Psycho* (1960) the shower-stabbing sequence is

Above: *A terrifying fire gag from a recent film. It has been calculated that 15 seconds is the longest that any stuntman can withstand a fire gag despite the effectiveness of protective clothing.* (*Kobal Collection*)

Right: *A scene from* The Towering Inferno *(1974), a film that combined fire, water and explosions. More than 200 stunts were performed yet no-one was hurt.* (*Kobal Collection*)

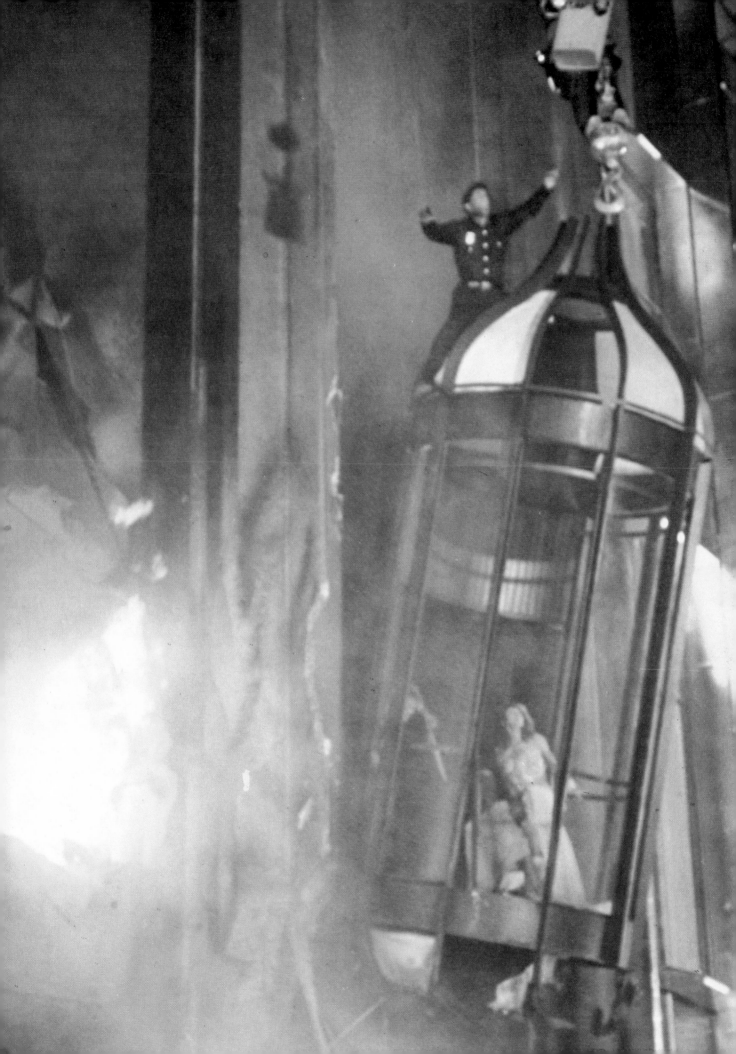

horrific in its implications rather than in what is actually shown. But with films such as *The Wild Bunch* (1969) the trend was set for more and more realistic effects. *Straw Dogs* (1971) features one particularly gruesome scene in which a man shoots himself in the foot with a shotgun. To achieve the effect of a severed foot, a boot was filled with steak and liberally sprinkled with fake blood, known in Britain as Kensington Gore. When the boot was exploded with squibs, the result was highly effective.

But spectacular effects such as this and the ones in *Bonnie and Clyde* (1968) are fairly easy to produce and involve little or no risk. Much harder to produce and potentially much more hazardous are fire and explosion sequences. In these the unpredictable is always possible and if it occurs the results can be fatal. Explosions demand skilful handling and part of a modern special effects man's rigorous training, in Hollywood anyway, includes a state-approved explosives course. One fairly common stunt is one in which a soldier is blown straight up into the air, perhaps as the result of standing on a mine. Obviously the stuntman cannot actually do this and it is here that cooperation between special effects department and stuntman comes in. Usually the stuntman jumps on a trampoline, masked either by an object or by being set just below the level of the ground. A charge is placed nearby and at the precise second that the stuntman jumps upwards, so the charge is detonated. The overall effect and safety depends on the split-second timing of the special effects man.

For mass explosion sequences, say in a battle, cone-shaped 'mortars' or 'pots' are placed in the ground. These are filled with 'flash' powder, Fuller's Earth, Bentonite, and various soft materials to create a cloud effect. The pots are connected by wires to a central board where they can be exploded severally or individually. Given that the explosions will occur in the midst of other action, careful preparation and attention to timing are vital.

If there is such a thing as the 'most dangerous stunt' it is probably the fire gag. Together with water, fire is the most unpredictable element to work with, and if the gag is combined with perhaps an exploding car or boat, the risks can be very high indeed. The modern fire suit consists of a special asbestos-padded suit, unflammable woollen gloves, a face mask moulded with the actor's features, and a miniature oxygen tank and breathing apparatus which enables the stuntman to breathe after being set alight. Over all this the stuntman wears ordinary clothes. When ready, the stuntman is doused with a carefully prepared mixture of alcohol and petrol, sometimes petrol-based jelly is used, and set alight. Fifteen seconds is the maximum time that any stuntman can bear the fire's heat, a record established in *Tobruk* (1967), and accidents are fairly common.

Two recent films that give some idea of the spectacular effects that can be created by stuntmen and special effects working in close liaison are *Earthquake* (1974) and *The Towering Inferno* (1974). *The Towering Inferno* features a massive blaze inside the world's largest building that traps a number of people in the nightclub at the top of the building. All attempts to extinguish the fire fail, and it is finally decided to explode the water tanks on the roof. More than two hundred individual stunts were performed, including several spectacular burnings, and some one million gallons (4 540 000 litres) of water were pumped onto the actors. What was amazing, and a credit to the sophistication of stunt techniques today, was that with strict safety precautions and absolute co-ordination and planning, no-one was hurt.

A chilling scene from The Invasion of the Body Snatchers *(1979) demonstrates why make-up and special effects departments in the film industry have earned themselves the reputation of being magicians. (United Artists)*